POLISHED

A Young Professional's Guide for Success

CALVIN PURNELL, JR.

BALBOA
PRESS
A DIVISION OF HAY HOUSE

Copyright © 2016 Calvin Purnell, Jr.

All rights reserved. No part of this book may be used or reproduced by any means, graphic, electronic, or mechanical, including photocopying, recording, taping or by any information storage retrieval system without the written permission of the author except in the case of brief quotations embodied in critical articles and reviews.

Balboa Press books may be ordered through booksellers or by contacting:

Balboa Press
A Division of Hay House
1663 Liberty Drive
Bloomington, IN 47403
www.balboapress.com
1 (877) 407-4847

Because of the dynamic nature of the Internet, any web addresses or links contained in this book may have changed since publication and may no longer be valid. The views expressed in this work are solely those of the author and do not necessarily reflect the views of the publisher, and the publisher hereby disclaims any responsibility for them.

The author of this book does not dispense medical advice or prescribe the use of any technique as a form of treatment for physical, emotional, or medical problems without the advice of a physician, either directly or indirectly. The intent of the author is only to offer information of a general nature to help you in your quest for emotional and spiritual well-being. In the event you use any of the information in this book for yourself, which is your constitutional right, the author and the publisher assume no responsibility for your actions.

Any people depicted in stock imagery provided by Thinkstock are models, and such images are being used for illustrative purposes only. Certain stock imagery © Thinkstock.

Print information available on the last page.

ISBN: 978-1-5043-5265-9 (sc)
ISBN: 978-1-5043-5267-3 (hc)
ISBN: 978-1-5043-5266-6 (e)

Library of Congress Control Number: 2016904201

Balboa Press rev. date: 03/18/2016

This book is dedicated to my children, Skylar, Calvin, III (Trey) and Brooklynn. The world is at your fingertips. You have the power to accomplish any goal you set your mind to achieve. But it requires work, dedication, discipline, sacrifice, and the possibility of losing some people along the way. If you do happen to leave behind some individuals, just know they were only with you for a season. Make sure you reflect on that connection to pull out the lessons of their existence with you. Focus on what you are working on at the present moment. Separate yourself from the end results. You don't want to rush through your process just to get to the end. You will want to cherish every moment spent working on your goals. There are lessons in the process for future use as you continue to work on new objectives. Your outcomes will come once the timing is perfect.

No one ever said your journey would be easy. Accomplishing goals can and will be hard at times. If you stay focused and determined, God will show you the way. Pray and ask Him for directions. Take the time to listen for God, as His messages will come in many forms. Be ready to receive them from people, music, signs, books, and your heart. God has your best interest, and He will not lead you down paths that are not for you. Learn the difference between your plan and His design for your life. He will make it plain for you to understand. Talk to God, tell Him what you want, and then go to work. Your efforts and focus will produce your outcomes in accomplishing any goal you set your mind, heart, and hands to find.

I love you.

CONTENTS

Acknowledgements ix
Introduction xi

Chapter 1   The Understanding 1
Chapter 2   Some Things My Parents Taught Me 5
Chapter 3   Character 7
Chapter 4   Appearance 13
Chapter 5   If You Become a Consultant 24
Chapter 6   Keep It Clean 28
Chapter 7   Mentors 31
Chapter 8   Building Relationships: Networking 34
Chapter 9   Speaking 43
Chapter 10 Diversity 50
Chapter 11 Work-Related Travel 55
Chapter 12 Study Your Environment 58
Chapter 13 Desire 60
Chapter 14 Focus 66
Chapter 15 Playing the Game 71
Chapter 16 Spirituality 76
Chapter 17 Self: My Notes To You 79
Chapter 18 Some Books I've Read 89
Chapter 19 A Few Pieces About Me 96

References 103

ACKNOWLEDGEMENTS

I'd like to give a special thank you to Tung To for allowing me to use his store, ToBox Men's Footwear Store, in Philadelphia for my cover photo shoot.

I owe credit to Chris Clark, president of Fiberlink, for the title of this book, as he once remarked that I appeared "polished." I also owe credit to Dan Price for staying on top of me to get this book done so he could review it while he was on his flight to his honeymoon.

INTRODUCTION

I have a few reasons behind writing this book. The first is simply my passion for writing and desire to help others grow.

When I started working at Fiberlink, I was the oldest person on the team, and I noticed the need for mentorship. I occasionally asked if they had mentors, and I wasn't surprised when they told me no. I began to pray about this book, and God told me this was the perfect time to #payitforward and produce a text to help young professionals along the way in their careers with my advice and personal experiences.

In the early stages of writing this book, I didn't have a title until my director, Jen LaPergola, one of my mentors, told me that the president of our company, Chris Clark, told her he thought I was "polished." As soon as I heard that, I knew what this book needed to be titled.

Chris Clark thinks I'm polished. I've heard that before from many people but never from a company president. Chris was the last person out of ten who I interviewed with at Fiberlink. That interview was more like a conversation with someone I've known for a period of time.

About two months after starting at Fiberlink, I had the chance to meet Chris again face-to-face. He stopped by my desk, and we had a twenty-minute conversation about my past experiences and family. I was then working out of both the Blue Bell (headquarters) and Philadelphia offices. Chris asked which one I liked the best. My answer was both, which is true. I think he thought I was bluffing, but I wasn't. Our Blue Bell office had a dynamic unlike the Philly workplace at the time. It was what I considered the brain trust. Philly was new and in the process of building up the teams. Being a bit older, I felt I would be a positive influence on the engineers in Philly. Since the team has been built, we now have our own brain trust.

I like working out of HQ because there's nothing like working in an office where the brain trust is. It also gives you the opportunity to have face time with people you wouldn't ordinarily see, and you can become known and not forgotten about. I like the Philly office because it is closer to home for me. Let's face it. I'm a Philly kid, born and raised. I love being in Center City. I feel like I'm home when I walk around down there.

I hope this book will give you some insight and guidance as you pursue your career and share your God-given talents with the world.

CHAPTER 1
THE UNDERSTANDING

I haven't designed this book to brag about my success. I want it to demonstrate the path I've taken to achievement, using my God-designed formula. Each of us has a success formula. With every accomplishment comes some form of struggle and occasional failure. Much of it comes from self-destruction or disruption in the process created for us. At times we put our hands in places they need not be, especially when God is working out His plan for our lives. Impatient, we think we can make people move in ways to give us what we want when only God can actually move those individuals so things can work out in our favor.

When we interfere with God's process, we often sabotage His work and efforts because we think we can do it better, which brings on those struggles and failures that fortunately provide lessons to apply to challenges that come later in life. The key component is paying attention to those teachings so you can teach others who are coming up the success ladder by paying it forward.

This concept, paying it forward, is something that everyone should adapt and apply to his or her life. Everyone needs some form of guidance and help along the way. If people tell you they did it all themselves, don't believe them. At some point in their lives, someone has taught them a lesson that helped them get to where they are now, whether it was a "Yes, I will help you" or a "No, I won't assist you."

Think back to a time when you started looking for a job or you were the new guy in the company. You needed someone to give you a chance so you could get your feet wet. Or you needed a task to complete to establish your presence in the organization so you could begin to earn others' trust and they could see that you knew what you were doing. Once that confidence is established, others will probably give you opportunities to proceed with your duties.

People need to give chances to those who are trying to establish themselves in their new positions. Everyone has to start as a new person someplace. We don't hit the ground running. Not everyone is aggressive about making others respect him or her and giving him or her a chance. Be the difference. Be the one who lends a helping hand to a new person coming on board. You were once a new employee in an organization and you will probably be one again at some point in your career.

Being a new employee can be a not-so-easy task for people. Don't be part of the standard. Just because everyone else on your team does not give new people a chance doesn't mean you have to follow suit. Be the leader. Take a risk, and give people guidance and direction. Someone was nice enough to give you an opportunity at some point. We need to be more encouraging to one another rather than discouraging.

On the flip side, being told no helps those who know how to accept no as an answer. No simply means "not now." It also means the person isn't the right individual to assist you. The word "no" helps you move someone out of your way so you can get to the right person.

For some, no is a showstopper. They take it to mean that it can't be done at all. If you have a God-given vision for something in your life, only you yourself can stop it. God gives us the vision and blueprint to perform the actions needed to bring forth what He has for us. If you do not follow the design, you cannot blame anyone but yourself. The right people will be there for you once the time is right. See the vision through. Make your connections. Build your relationships and, most importantly, share. Do not be the person with your hand out all the time. People will remember that about you. Success is not a hobby. It's a lifestyle.

When I was a child, my dad always talked to me about starting my own business. In that business, he wanted a do-nothing office in the building. He would say, "When people ask you what that office is for, you will say, 'That's my dad's do-nothing office.' When they ask you what I do in there, you will say, 'Nothing.'"

I haven't started my own business just yet, and I'm not sure that I will. But if I do, I will definitely get my dad his do-nothing office.

Over the years I've created an invisible council that I occasionally tap into to guide me along the way. Some might think it is a bit crazy, weird, or stupid. I, on the other hand, consider it simply genius. I call my invisible council "my board of directors." It includes the Holy Trinity, Glover (Pop), Jessie (Mom), Riddick (my grandparents), Upsher Purnell (my pop-pop), Napoleon Hill, Thich Nhat Hanh, and Eckhart Tolle.

Each directs me in different areas of my life via books they have written and lectures they have given. I use their past and present teachings to guide me in decisions I need to make. They provide clarity in circumstances and situations I come across, and they simply act as a helping hand. I also tap into my "other self," as Napoleon Hill calls it.

If you don't have an invisible council, I suggest you start building one of those who have been successful in life and once walked your path, which may not be exact but similar. They have left directions and clues as to how you too can become successful. But it's up to you to do the research.

CHAPTER 2
SOME THINGS MY PARENTS TAUGHT ME

Growing up my parents provided me with nuggets to carry throughout life. Sometimes I felt like a record was on repeat. As I began experiencing life, I realized my mom and dad was setting me up for success with their words of wisdom. Being young and inexperienced, I thought they didn't know anything, especially when it came to matters of the heart. As the years passed and to date I would hear my parents' voices telling me the following truths I needed as I venture down my life's path.

- Believe in God.
- Say your prayers and have faith that God will provide.
- Choose your friends wisely.
- Not everyone who smiles at you is your friend.

- Everyone who offers you advice is not your friend.
- If you're not certain about something, ask questions.
- Be a leader, not a jerk.
- Nothing is beneath a leader.
- Never look down your nose at people.
- Think before making decisions and speaking.
- Learn from your mistakes as well as from other people's errors.
- Always have more than one way to make money, but stick to your original plan.
- Don't wear your heart on your sleeve.
- If you get your house in order, everything else will come in line.
- Surround yourself with people of like minds but different sets of wisdom.
- Engage with people who are smarter than you are. You just might learn something.
- Use your head for something besides a hat rack.
- Never settle for less than what you already have unless the Spirit leads you to take a few steps backward to get a few steps forward.
- Not every lesson is given to you once. Often those same lessons will be repeated.

CHAPTER 3
CHARACTER

Here are a few questions to ask yourself:

1. Who am I?
2. Who am I when no one is watching?
3. What do I stand for?
4. What are my life's passions?
5. What do I believe in?
6. Who do I surround myself with?
7. How do I handle failure?
8. How do I handle victory?

Here are my answers at this point in my life to those questions:

1. I am Calvin Purnell Jr., a man who tries his best to honor God and help others along the way.
2. I am a thinker and a big-time mirror dancer, and I am working on creating a better me.

3. I stand for awareness and mindfulness.
4. I am passionate about motivating others and myself.
5. I believe in God and myself. I trust that He has my best interests at heart.
6. I surround myself with winners in life.
7. I receive the lessons of failure and find the blessings within them.
8. I am sometimes humble and arrogant when I am the victor. (I am trying to make that a full-time humility practice, but I'm still human, so I have work to do.)

Notice that I began the answers with "I am" or "I." Once you do that, you speak your intention into existence and give it life. This allows the universe to start sending it your way. The Bible says, "The tongue has the power of life and death, and those who love it will eat its fruit" (Prov. 18:21) (NIV). We are only speaking life, so be careful with your words.

Let's get back to character. The above questions are a good place to start when you are strengthening your character. I say "strengthening" because, at this point in your life, you should have started developing your character. You develop character through social activity and your interactions with others. It is also developed when no one is watching, or so you think. Remember that someone is always observing.

By design, we all have character, including those flaws within. There's no getting around that. Once you discover who you are, you begin to strengthen your character and awaken to your flaws. You can try to fix those faults, especially those that affect others and yourself negatively. But most importantly you should fix them to strengthen your character.

Understanding who you are is key. You don't want anyone else to define who you are. You should do it yourself. Welcome yourself to the world and say, "This is who I am but am not limited to."

Not restricting yourself is important. It shows that you are not limiting yourself to who you are, and that's that. Who you are changes as you grow. For example, you change because your thoughts, lifestyle, and beliefs adapt. You get the picture.

When I was about twenty-two or twenty-three years old, I was so immature, thinking I had my life all mapped out until my circumstances and priorities changed. I figured I knew who I was, and I was proud to beat my chest and say, "This is who I am. Take it or leave it." I was so undeveloped.

Circumstances and priorities change. Therefore, you adapt. Your character and your flaws transform. Maybe I should say that you are awakened to your flaws that have not been exposed until now.

Take time for yourself multiple times a week to learn who you are and how your heart and mind are wired. Those moments are precious and vital for you. It gives you the opportunity to study how your life affects others and how to build self-worth. Time alone also gives you the interval to understand how you impact yourself. Yes, yourself. We can be a detriment to ourselves if we don't take control. You have to look out for your own well-being, mind, heart, body, and soul.

Mike Zimmerman wrote an article, "Ties That Bind," in *Success Magazine* on Denzel Washington. A phrase that Denzel used—and I quoted below—stuck with me and hit home due to how I carry myself. "I don't take myself seriously, but I take my work seriously." Mike Zimmerman says, "That's how Denzel describes his relationship with himself" (November 2012). I got from that quote that he's humbled by life's experiences and has fun in his personal life and just goes with it. On the professional side of his life, he ensures he handles his business in a professional manner at all times.

Within your character comes an ego. Everyone has one. Remember that, if your ego is too big, it kills your talent. Be humble as it shows others that you care and you've been through something in life that slowed you down to give you time to think about your actions before causing reactions.

People will remember you for your compassion toward yourself and others. Then you have those who have the character trait of saving themselves first and placing the blame on others. Throwing people under the bus to save yourself when you are wrong makes you wrong as well. People will look at that and judge your character based on that incident.

In a work environment, each person should come together to resolve all conflicts. If it is a simple issue of not liking someone, simply put your feelings to the side and work together. That's your purpose for being at work, simply to work. No one is there to make friends. Don't get me wrong. There's nothing wrong with making friends at work. The bottom line is to produce for your organization as a whole.

People might not like you for a number of reasons, which might have nothing to do with work at all. They could be personal even though you never did anything to them. For example:

1. It could be the color of your skin.
2. Maybe you replaced their friend in the position you currently hold.
3. They might think you aren't a good fit for the job.
4. Or you filled the position they really wanted.

The reasons vary. What you need to know is that it's none of your business why a person dislikes you. Do your job to the best of your ability and with integrity, professionalism, and the highest level of quality. All should be your main objective. If you encounter issues in the workplace, make sure to keep a paper trail of your conversations and discussions by putting things in writing. It may come in handy later, especially if you find yourself in a "he-said/she-said" situation.

If you are wrong, have some dignity about yourself. Own your mistakes as you would your successes. Being able to admit your wrongs will always gain you respect from others. People will respect and trust your word. And without respect and trust, your relationships will never grow.

Always display good character. When starting a new job, don't be that guy who tries to become too familiar too soon, the one who thinks he or she knows it all when he or she has a lot to learn about the culture of the new team and organization he or she has joined.

> If conversations happen via email and your organization deletes messages after a certain period of time, be sure to print your proof and store it someplace safe just in case you need to provide proof of the actions you've taken if someone states otherwise. Or save a tree. Just archive the emails on a hard drive or USB key.

Take your time to get to know people. Don't throw yourself at others and force your personality on them. If you do, most of your colleagues will not like you for that very reason. Sit back and assess your new environment. Focus on learning your new role. Get an understanding of who does what in the organization. Find out who can get you answers to the questions you have. Get an understanding of the inner workings of the teams and find out how you can add value to them. You were brought on because you impressed the hiring manager. Don't make that person regret adding you to the team.

Invest in yourself and take some courses in professionalism. Or find a mentor to help groom these specific skills. There are plenty of resources—articles, books, seminars, and people—who are willing to help you grow. Research and reach out to them. You can contact me if you like. I would be willing to help you develop. And once you feel comfortable enough, make sure you #payitforward and help someone else transform. We all need a helping hand.

CHAPTER 4
APPEARANCE

Take pride in your appearance. Figure out your signature look and own it! Get yourself measured so you can purchase clothes that fit you properly. If you need something altered, go to a great tailor to get stitched up.

I built a relationship with Steve of Steve's Olde City Tailoring and Dry Cleaning in Philadelphia. Steve is an expert at his craft. I purchase off-the-rack suits, and he makes them look like they were made specifically for me. For example, Steve taught me, when getting your slacks hemmed, always ask for a blind stitch as it keeps the hem line invisible. Trust me. It truly makes a difference.

I enjoy getting dressed every day. Even on the days I don't feel like it, I make sure I'm fresh. I'm not bragging. I just take pride in my appearance. You never know who you will meet, your next employer, a new business associate, or your next boyfriend or girlfriend. Always be ready. Take the time to prepare yourself before walking out of your home. Make sure your hair is styled the way you like it and your nails are trimmed and cleaned. Ladies, if wearing makeup is a part of your look, ensure it's applied properly. If you wear lipstick, verify it's not smeared on your teeth. Some people will let you walk around and talk to others without informing you of your mishap.

Check your shoes for dirt, dust, and residue from spills. Take a cloth to remove any stains that might exist. If you don't get your shoes shined, polish them yourself. A polished/shined shoe will set you apart from the rookies who think they are making some noise with those run-down shoes and blended fabric suits.

Speaking of suits, stick with wool. Polyester rayon blends are a no-go because they look cheap. If you're unfamiliar with the differences in fabrics, find an image consultant to get an understanding of the different types of blends. My friend Brian Lipstein, owner of Henry A. Davidsen Master Tailors & Image Consultants in Philadelphia, has a great service that he offers to assist men in getting their image perfected. Visit his website at www.henrydavidsen.com. Brian takes the time to understand what you like and what you are looking for when it comes to your clothing. He wants to make sure you are putting your money in the right place when purchasing from him.

I've met with some image consultants who just want you to spend your money in their shop regardless of whether you really want or need the items. Brian sets himself apart and really takes pride in building a relationship with his clients so he can provide them with the items they are truly looking for. Wherever you are located, find and build a relationship with a tailor and/or image consultant. It will change your life.

When buying suits, purchase those that lay on you properly based on your shape. It's important to know the difference between what looks good on you and what you like. Just because you like it doesn't mean it will look good on you. Once you find your style, you will know it personally because you will feel good in it. You will feel like the world has no hold on you and life is as perfect as it can be. Ladies and gentlemen, the stamp of approval is when an older woman who is well put together compliments you on your appearance.

Here's a tip about off-the-rack suits. Make sure you take a small cutting utensil and open your pockets. If you didn't know, the pockets are stitched closed. Also take the thread out on the vents of the suit jacket. These are the openings on the back of the suit jacket. Finally do not make the rookie mistake I made in 1996 when I was contracting for Johnson & Johnson by leaving the labels on the sleeve of the suit jacket. It was the first suit I ever purchased for myself, and I was excited. I just knew I was doing something by leaving the label on that sleeve. Thank God Alain pulled me to the side and helped me out.

He said, "Let me tell you something. Never leave the label on the sleeve of your suit jacket. It looks

This is my personal opinion and not a rule of any guideline that I've ever read. In professional environments, Monday through Thursday is business attire days. I think your shirts should exclude deep, dark, solid colors like royal blue, purple, brown, black, hot pink, and so forth. Those hue of shirts remind me of a young adult hanging out in the clubs. Learn how to keep your business attire separate from your hanging-out gear. If you go with colors, ensure they are soft hues. When in business settings, try your best to look the part. And yes, dress for the position you want and not the role you are in. Your career is as serious as you take it. You might as well take your attire earnestly too.

Fridays in most organizations is dress-down day. Feel free to wear your dark color shirts that day. And be sure to keep your buttons done. You are still at work. No one wants to see any cleavage, chest hairs, or gold or silver chains. Remember that you are still in your place of business.

tacky, and it's a rookie mistake. Don't ever say I never gave you some helpful information."

I was somewhat embarrassed but also happy Alain helped me out. I could have walked around looking like a young fool all day had he not told me that tidbit of very useful information. This is why we must all #payitforward to assist someone out along the way.

You don't want a frumpy look. Anyone can have one, no matter his or her size. What stands out most is if your clothes are too big or small. Most people look at your clothes before they observe you. I personally start from the shoes up. If your shoes are well taken care of, shined, and not run over and your heels are in good shape, I know you take pride in your appearance.

Wrinkles in your clothes also stand out. My grandma taught me that it's important to press your outfits. Even if it's a T-shirt, press it. You would be surprised at how a wrinkled T-shirt shows through the dress shirt.

I've had many coworkers over the course of my career tell me that I look nice or appear like I just left the runway. I believe it is important to present yourself properly. Regardless of your position, you should dress to impress. Care about your appearance and the way that others view you. Remember the old faithful statement: dress for your next position.

You never know where you will meet your next employer or person who might recommend you for an opportunity. It's important to leave a lasting first impression on people from your appearance, communication skills, and your work performance. I have a few more tips, but those stand out the most for me. As time goes on, you will create your own lasting impression points that you take personally.

Polished

Choose the right color shoe to wear with your dresses, skirts, slack, or suits:

Shoe Color	Outfit Color
Black and Brown	Navy
Black and Brown	Mid-grey
Black	Charcoal
Brown	Brown
Black and Brown	Black

I have a tip for you about brand-new shoes: Before you wear them, take them to a trusted cobbler to have him or her strip the factory polish from the shoes and shine to your liking. Also get taps on the heel and toe of the shoes to preserve the soles. You just spent your hard-earned money on some new kicks. You'll want them to last as long as possible.

Keep an eye on the taps. They wear down, and you'll want to replace them when necessary. Also keep an eye on the sole. Over time they will also wear down. You can have the sole replaced along with the heel to preserve the shoe if you don't have them tapped. That will also save you a few bucks on replacing your shoes due to wear and tear.

If you happen to purchase your shoes from a discount retailer, be sure to check the sole for price tags. Remove the tags before you wear your new shoes. Nothing looks tackier than seeing someone walking down the street with a price tag still on the bottom of his or her shoe.

Take care of your shoes. When I work in the city, I get my shoes shined once a week at the shoe repair shop on 17th and Ranstead Street in Philadelphia. I own several shoes and do not wear the same pair regularly. So I figured I need to take the time to treat my shoes right. I go to the same person each time. His name is Mike.

I use the time that I'm getting my shoes shined to decompress. I just sit back in the chair and relax for a few moments. I take deep breaths, and sometimes I even meditate to clear my mind. It's a great midweek refresher.

When it comes to your barber or hairstylist, it's important to build a relationship with him or her so he or she knows what you like and how to style your hair. A very good friend of mine, Shawn (Shizz) Porter is a barber in Los Angeles. His salon, II Fifteen Exclusive Men's Salon & Spa at 6103 Melrose Avenue,[1] caters to many celebrities. He has a huge clientele across the world. If the celebrities aren't local, once they fly into LA, they make sure they have an appointment booked with Shizz.

Shizz specializes in the art of grooming and takes pride in making sure he understands what his clients want and need when he is cutting their hair. Oftentimes, if they aren't deciding to switch up their haircuts, Shizz already knows how to style their hair. He was featured in an article written by Rhett Butler, "Era of the Gentleman: Upscale Grooming Is the New Trend Among Men of All Ages."[2]

If you're ever in LA and want that special treatment, look him up and make an appointment. Let Shizz know that I sent you. You will not be disappointed. In fact Shizz is the only barber that I let cut my hair. And since he's in LA and I'm in Philly, I just do it myself.

Ladies and gentlemen, please pay attention to your fingernails. Men, keep your fingernails cut short and clean. Nothing looks more unkempt than a man with dirt under his fingernails. I personally shake a lot of hands throughout my

---

[1] This translates to 215 for Philly's area code.
[2] Rhett Butler, "Era of the Gentleman: Upscale Grooming Is the New Trend Among Men of all Ages, *Jet* (February 15, 2010).

day. If I see dirt under someone's nails, guess whose hand I am no longer shaking? You guessed it! That person right there!

Ladies, if you wear fingernail polish, inspect your polish before you go to bed at night. If you have chips, remove the polish from your nails and reapply if you choose to. The same goes for your toenails. If you wear shoes that expose your toes, make sure your polish is not chipped. Men and ladies should visit their favorite nail salon and treat themselves to a manicure and/or pedicure. There's nothing wrong with a little me time. We all need it occasionally.

Build a relationship with people you use for services. They get to know you and understand your style and what you like. Once people get to know you, they tend to take care of you based on your likes. And make sure you tip the person providing you a service properly. And if you choose to maintain yourself, please keep up the maintenance as needed.

When people think about clothes, most figure they are going to spend a lot. But you don't have to. You can shop for bargains. I do it all the time. I shop in the off-season to get the best deals on items that are overpriced anyway. You want to get the most for your dollar. I hit the clearance racks in stores. So what if they are last year's items? If you like it and get a good price, buy it!

I also shop online at www.overstock.com, www.ruelala.com, www.gilt.com, www.bananarepublic.com, Nordstrom, Nordstrom Rack, and wherever I can find a deal. And if you're in Philadelphia, check out A Man's Imagine on East Passyunk Avenue. Ask for Lou or Mario. Tell them Calvin sent you.

You will never know the labels I wear because I don't purchase the cookie-cutter uniform items that stores place on mannequins. If you purchase that look and live and/or work in a metropolitan area, you are guaranteed to see about six people wearing your outfit. And if you're lucky, it might even be on the same day you are wearing it.

Mix and match labels. Have fun with it. Break the rules of matching everything. Don't go overboard to the point where people are looking at you weird. Make it just enough so people are observing you with envy, sort of like they wished they thought about putting together outfits like that. The point of wearing clothes is so people can look at you. Make it worth it!

I am guilty of going on Pinterest to find styles I like. Once I find a look that I like, I start pulling similar pieces out of my closet to make my very own look for less. Check out my boards on Pinterest. I have a board called "My Style! Simply Cal." With everything pinned on that board, I either put together a similar outfit from my closet or plan on doing it. Remember that it is life, so have fun with your clothes!

I have some words of advice. If you don't like how you look in it, don't wear it. It probably doesn't look right on you anyway. Many people force styles on themselves and look uncomfortable in it. Watch yourself in the mirror. If your first thought is, *This isn't me*, take it off and start over. You want to make sure you are comfortable in your clothes.

It's not a competition. Dress with your personal style. Don't worry about what others are wearing. And don't fret about the comments that others might make about your attire. Dress appropriately. Men, wear undershirts. Ladies, wear camisoles if your shirt is low cut. Men, if you have on a dress shirt and go tieless, wear a V-neck T-shirt. If you go with a crew neck and it shows, you just killed your look, and now you look sloppy, as if you don't care about your appearance.

Don't wear graphic T-shirts, as they will show through your dress shirt. The last thing you want someone to see is your graphic prints under a nice shirt. Trust me. It will show, and it will throw off your entire outfit.

Ladies, pay close attention to the weather forecast for the day. If the meteorologist says it's going to be a windy day, do not wear that pretty, flowing skirt. The wind will blow that skirt up, and your backside and front will get exposed for everyone around you to see. That is the last thing you will want to happen to you. I've seen it happen plenty of times, and it causes a great deal of embarrassment for those women.

If you do wear a skirt and the wind is blowing, be sure to hold it down with your hands to possibly prevent any problems. Or wear some form of shorts underneath so your unmentionables are not fully exposed if the wind does blow a gust up your skirt.

Also refrain from wearing form-fitting clothing as it will bring negative attention to you. There will be that one man or woman bold enough to tell you how sexy you look. It might be wanted or unwanted attention. If it's wanted, leave that crap outside the workplace and go hang out in a bar or club with those tight clothes on. If it's unwanted, the best thing you can do for yourself is to not wear those form-fitting clothes at all as it will be a distraction to everyone in the workplace. People will talk about you in a bad way, for example,

> Did you see so-and-so today? I can't believe he or she wore those tight clothes. He or she might as well have nothing on because you can see every curve and angle ... Did you see so-and-so today? He or she is looking good! You can see everything he or she owns with those tight clothes on! You have to go see for yourself!

You don't want to be the talk of the workplace, so avoid it at all costs.

For the cold days, purchase a few overcoats, black and brown (dark brown and camel or khaki as some call it) and maybe a navy. I recommend both full-length and three-quarter length coats. Full-length coats will help keep your legs warm on those extremely cold days. Three-quarter length coats are for the not so cold days. Nothing looks worse than an individual walking around on a thirty-degree day in the middle of his or her metropolitan district in a suit without an overcoat. Not only will wearing an overcoat keep you warm, it will complement your polished look.

Carry an umbrella for rainy days as it will keep you and your clothes dry. The last thing you want is an unkempt look. Paying attention to the weather states that you care about your well-being. If you carry a bag, purchase a small umbrella for those days you might have forgotten your regular one. Or keep an emergency one in the office. Sometimes the meteorologists are wrong about forecasts. Mother Nature does what she wants. That is very true. I've seen it rain on days they said it was supposed to be sunny.

When it comes to appearance, your health and hygiene are also major factors. Stay on top of your health. Schedule doctor's visits for checkups

Practice umbrella etiquette when walking down the street. If your umbrella is on the larger side, like one used for golf, pay attention to the people you approach. Tilt your umbrella to the side so it does not hit anyone, or raise it higher than the other people in your area as you pass them. Remember that life isn't just about you. Think about others' well-being, and treat people how you want to be treated.

If your large umbrella bumps someone's smaller umbrella, somebody will get wet. Not everyone will care, but if you do, others will notice and learn from your actions. And they just might care the next time they are in that situation to make an adjustment with their umbrellas. #payitforward.

and having your labs checked. Get all of your blood work done to make sure you are in tip-top condition. If you're not, ensure you are taking the proper actions to work toward getting back to good health.

Hygiene is important. Use soap and water to wash your body. Use deodorant and floss, brush your teeth, and use mouthwash. If you're a naturalist, remember that you don't work alone. However you choose to keep yourself clean, do your colleagues a favor and stay on top of it. No one wants to smell body odor. And no one wants to reek of too much cologne or perfume either. When applying your cologne or perfume, think of your colleagues who might have allergies. Please be cognizant of your scents and body odors.

If you haven't found your personal style, I suggest you do. Style is different from fashion. Style is your timeless imprint on yourself that is your own. I do not mean "own" as in you have purchased it. In this definition, "own" is defined as your taste in the selection of your appearance. Take the time to find what you like and what looks best on you from your hairstyle, facial hair, and/or makeup. What about your clothes? It even comes down to your weight. What size do you feel you're at your best? Once you discover that, exercise to maintain it because you will spend a lot of money over time on your style, and you don't want to waste it.

Remember that appearance is all about attention to details.

CHAPTER 5
IF YOU BECOME A CONSULTANT

B e the best! Essentially be better than the full-time employees. Be humble. Be a quiet storm that moves mountains. Let's face it. Your employer came looking for you due to the need for greater expertise that their full-time employees might not possess. You have to uncover the organization's needs so you can remain a needed resource.

Yes, there are times when companies choose to cut costs so they bring in consultants. Your aim should be to make yourself invaluable and guarantee the employer knows they cannot live without you. The plan is to have your contract renewed at the end of your term because the big picture is a stream of revenue in your pocket.

It is very important to separate yourself from the full-time employees. You must represent your consulting company at all times. I'm not saying that you don't talk to the full-time employees. Keep your mind focused on the business. Friendships are for outside the workplace. Keep it that way if you happen to be acquaintances with some of them. If they are truly your friends, they will understand that your time in that company is valuable and you are there to perform a job.

Lunch, office hangouts, and water cooler talk is not something you are to participate in. Go to lunch alone. Say hello and good-bye. And get your water, coffee, or tea and keep it moving. Don't get caught up in idle conversations. If you happen to comment on certain things, it can be used against you, and now you've lost your contract.

Dress professionally, no matter the corporate culture. You are not an employee of that company. You should represent your firm in a professional manner at all times. That includes Friday when many organizations have a casual day—unless the direct supervisor of your firm tells you otherwise. But I still say wear business attire.

If you make the decision to become a consultant, find an organization with long-lasting or several contracts. If your project ends, you might be able to roll into another contract that the company holds.

Additionally you need to pay attention to the life of the contract. Know when it is scoped to end. If that time is approaching and you don't see the client extending the contract, be proactive, that is, speak to your project manager or whomever you report to and ensure you can have another opportunity lined up. You need to make sure you do not have a break in pay. I'm quite sure you have monthly bills you are responsible for.

If your project happens to end and you do not have another opportunity lined up, find out if your firm has bench pay, that is, when you are paid a portion or entire regular salary while between projects. Not all firms offer that. So do your homework before signing up. You don't want to be surprised if your contract is not extended and you end up with no paycheck coming in. Always be in the know.

If you choose to move out of a role to get different experiences, you might have that option if you are working for a large or well-represented firm. Understand that you can be terminated from a contract at any time. Most of them are at-will contracts, that is, you can leave or be terminated at any time.

Also pay attention to non-compete clauses that you more than likely will have to sign when taking on a contract role. Read it well. There is a possibility that you cannot work for another company, filling the same role with the same client. Or you might not be able to work for a competitor for a year or more after leaving the company. Do your homework on non-competes.

When it comes to your résumé, be sure to name the consulting company you work for, not the client's name. You don't work for the client; you work for the firm, which is an entity of its own. They deserve their respect on your résumé. I don't care if the client is a well-known organization whose name precedes them. You don't work for them. If a reference check is done and it is found out that the organization did not employ you, you just blew your opportunity over wanting false recognition of employment. If it is that important to you to name that organization on your résumé, use the following example:

ABC Llc. Philadelphia, PA 2010–2015

Business Consultant, Contracted to XYZ, Inc.

That will give your firm the respect they deserve, and you will have satisfied your need to name the client.

Finally, if your firm places you on a 1099 form with the IRS, you are basically being paid straight cash without any tax deductions. Find an accountant, and let him or her know your salary. He or she will be able to tell you how much you need to send to the IRS and state every time you get paid.

Do not try to shortchange Uncle Sam. Trust me. It's not worth it. The IRS and state will track you down if you owe them money. It will not go away; nor will they ignore it.

CHAPTER 6
KEEP IT CLEAN

Social Media

Do your best to refrain from social media activity while at work. Many employers are very active on social media for a number of reasons. One reason is to see how many of their employees are utilizing work hours to play around on the Internet. Facebook, Instagram, Twitter, and many of the like are possibly being monitored. If you are active on those sites, just know that you are stealing time. You will have plenty of time after work to be active on those sites.

Understand those social media accounts are yours, but they are not private. Posting certain content in your private time can come back to haunt you. Do not post things about your employer or coworkers online. If a colleague or mutual friend sees your post, someone is sure to tell others. The word will spread like wildfire. And if you do post something of the sort, best believe that someone simply clicking a screenshot has captured the post. If you happen to delete a post, someone else may have it now. Keep that in the back of your mind at all times.

The best practice is to not vent online about work or personal information.

Office Romance

It happens all the time. There are several good-looking people at work, but there are more attractive people outside. Flirting with an office mate can take one of three turns—a good relationship, a bad commitment, and/or termination of employment. Sometimes they work; other times they don't. I'm not here to tell you not to do it. I'm just advising you to think long and hard about it.

Office romances work out occasionally. But other times they don't. They make for awkward situations if someone's feelings get hurt. Keep it clean. Try your best to leave your love options outside the office.

Mental and physical attractions happen. At times there's no getting around it. Control is the key. Let me restate that. Self-control is the key. It takes work to control your emotions, and it's worth it. One thing to consider is your career. If you value your success, you will practice self-control. If you don't, you can land you and your career into an automatic decline, especially if the word gets out and the wrong people get a hold of this information.

Also consider rumors that might surface about you and the other person. Rumors never turn out to be good. They get flipped and turned around to spin the truth. What is worse are rumors about women. Men tend to look good when talking about their sex life unless women spin up the rumors that he's no good in bed. But rumors about women sleeping around with their coworkers give them a bad name. So have some respect for yourself and the women in your office. Think about how you would feel if those rumors were spread around about your mother, sister, or daughter. Either way, ladies and gentlemen, you should respect your reputation and everyone you interact with.

If you happen to have an encounter with a coworker, keep it to yourself. Even if he or she tells others, still keep it to yourself. Remember that your reputation is also on the line. People remember how you handle situations. To be on the safe side, be like a former coworker of mine who referred to avoiding office romances by having on blinders. Stay focused on the job, not those individuals looking for a good time.

There! The problem is solved!

CHAPTER 7
MENTORS

The first thing to know about a mentor-mentee relationship is the mentor learns from the mentee just as well. When someone is mentoring you, his or her first efforts should be to build up your faith in him or her to mentor you. Faith is the foundation of building up anything in life for anyone. Although you are watching them before, you should have silently built the faith before the relationship began.

Choose your mentors wisely. If someone offers to mentor you, be sure this person will add value to your growth as a professional. It is okay to decline someone's offer, just as well as it is appropriate for someone to decline your request to be mentored by him or her. It must be the right match for both parties.

A mentor has accomplished similar goals you are looking to obtain. Your objectives do not have to be perfectly aligned, but it should make sense. I have mentors who are not in my same career path, but they have strengths in areas where I need guidance.

Once someone catches your attention and you think that person would be a good mentor to you, pay closer attention to him or her. Observe him or her as much as you can so it gives you the opportunity to see if this person is a good match for you.

Take notes. If you decide to ask for this person to mentor you, you want to be prepared to answer questions as to why you want him or her to mentor you. This individual might be flattered at first. Then he or she might begin to wonder why you are choosing him or her. Once the question of why comes your way, you will be prepared to tell him or her exactly why you want him or her to mentor you. This will give the person something to think about. It also shows him or her that you've done your homework and are willing to work for "food." If your request is granted, your new mentor will be feeding you valuable information.

You want him or her to know that he or she will not be wasting time on someone who is just looking for a free ride or information. Be prepared to give back to your mentor. This relationship is just like any other. It's not take-take-take. It is a give-and-take for both parties involved. Everyone has value to add to relationships. So be prepared to give back.

Don't be afraid to have an opposite sex mentor. I have a few female mentors who have groomed me in ways that my male mentors have not. For example, one of my female mentors, Carolyn Madison, told me it's always important to dress for the role you are looking to fill. Appearance is the first thing people see. Employers look to see how well you present yourself. If a new role becomes available, you always want to be the person that managers think of as a great fit. Carolyn also told me repeatedly that I am just as smart as the next person and I can have any job I want as long as I apply myself.

Be diverse with your mentor selections. Mentors of different races can teach you cultural differences that your same race cannot. Many people are ignorant to racial boundaries, and it is very important to know them. It is critical to know your audience. It is also significant to not assume everyone is the same. Just because the race appears to be the same does not mean they are. Those individuals can come from different sides of the tracks. One could have grown up as very fortunate in the suburbs; the other could have grown up in an urban area and had to work harder to receive achievements. The above statements speak to all races of the world, no matter where they come from. So be diverse. It will help you grow even further in your life and professional experiences.

Finally this is something I exercise regularly after years of being mentored and listening to others. Mentor yourself as well. By doing so, you have to listen to your inner voice and trust yourself with the choices and decisions you make for your life. Nobody makes you do anything. People can influence you, but ultimately you make the final decision.

CHAPTER 8
BUILDING RELATIONSHIPS: NETWORKING

If you don't have a LinkedIn profile or some other professional social media profile, create one. LinkedIn is just my preference. These sites will be a driving force to building professional relationships. Take these profiles seriously. They are not the playground like other social media sites. Keep it clean and professional at all times.

One of the keys to success in your career will reside in your ability to build and maintain relationships with people. This factor will help you in more ways than one throughout your career. Someone you've connected with may end up being your link to your next career move. Better yet, since you've adapted to the #payitforward method, you might be the connection to someone you've built a relationship with for his or her next career move.

Did you know your network started when you were a child? You've made friends and associates throughout the years of schooling and in the neighborhoods where you grew up in. It is very important to reach out to the people you connected with as far back as grade school. If you remember their names but are not sure where they are, use social media, for example, Facebook, Twitter, LinkedIn, and a host of other social media sites. Almost everyone has at least one of the social media accounts. Reach out to reconnect and see what they are up to. Tell them what you've been doing. Try not to sound like you are bragging. Humble yourself, and offer ways to help them grow their network or advance their careers. And also see what they can do to help you. This requires you to fully listen to what they are saying to you when they are telling you what they've been up to. Take notes during the conversation so you can remember the parts that stick out the most and find out what will benefit you. Additionally hear what they are saying to you so you can find ways to assist them with your connections and experiences.

In December 2012, I became a member of a networking group called National Guys Night Out (GNO) (www.nationalguysnightout.com) in Philadelphia. Unfortunately this group has disbanded due to the leader accepting a new position within his organization in a different part of the United States.

GNO was a group of guys who came together every second Wednesday of every month to discuss business, network, talk sports, and enjoy a drink. I became a member to build my network and build trusted relationships with well-established men from various industries. GNO was a great group of men who were of like minds and willing to help each other. This group was not your typical networking group where people come to force a product they are selling. These guys came together each month, even if they did not generate business. We learned what each person did and sent referrals when it made sense.

I also enjoyed that this group was all guys. We didn't have that added element of females that could cause some pressures that men get regularly. The added element to impress a female did not exist with this group. I eventually became an ambassador of GNO in December 2013. It was a great honor to be considered as a valued member and resource of that great organization.

I think it is important to network constantly. Even if you do not become a member of a networking group, it is critical to build your network.

One afternoon I had lunch with my friend Brian Propp, the Philadelphia Flyers legend. He was then the vice president of strategic account management at the Judge Group. We were discussing mentoring and networking to help young professionals. Brian mentioned the importance of attending networking events and how it gives individuals the opportunity to meet a bunch of people in one place at one time. It sounds simple, but it has a heavy impact on expanding your network.

When I attend networking events, I make sure to acknowledge the host first, if I know him or her personally. Then I catch up with people I know. This establishes a presence as I work the room of people I know. It makes the individuals I do not know wonder who I am. We catch up and share some laughs. Now I've established that I am a person whom others need to meet.

Now I introduce myself to the people I do not know. We exchange cards and establish a common ground. Then I let them know that I am willing to help them in any way possible, whether it is to introduce them to someone I know who can possibly help them or if I can help them myself. Make your meeting them be about them. Be genuine. If you do not plan to help someone, don't offer your help. It will come out in the wash at some point that you did not intend to help. So don't make a fool of yourself by extending your hand and pulling it back once someone reaches out to you.

If you meet someone whom you have no commonality with, introduce him or her to someone you know in the room. That breaks your contact with them for the moment. It also opens the door for someone else to connect with him or her and establish an opportunity to help each other. In my eyes, no connection is a bad association. Someone always knows someone who needs help. If the connection is not good for you, it might be beneficial for someone you know.

Drop yourself in a place where you don't know anyone and meet four or five people. Figure out how you can add value to their lives. It doesn't have to be a networking event. It can be a happy hour, restaurant, or seminar of your interests. It doesn't always have to be business related. A friend's party will do too.

When building relationships, make sure you add value to that association. People will remember that about you and look out for you when something crosses their paths that reminds them of you. This person will add value to your life and the relationship the two of you are building.

Everyone needs help or knows someone who needs assistance in some area of his or her life. We do not get to where we are by ourselves. Someone has helped us, so it is imperative to pay it forward.

If you have selfish tendencies, get rid of them. This quality will get you nowhere in life. It might work for a short period of time, but people will recognize your ways. Individuals in your network will talk about it, and you will probably lose help from others.

If you focus on building relationships, you will construct your network. I've made the mistake of networking to get something out of others with very little to offer in the early stage of my career. I was looking for a job fresh out of school with zero technical experience. Someone told me to network. So I did. I met new people who were in positions I wanted to be in and those who could have clearly hired me.

But I had nothing to offer, or so I thought. The only experience I had was education and my years of working at McDonald's. Most companies wanted new hires to have at least two to three years of experience. So someone I met asked me what I had to offer. All I could suggest (or so I thought) was my five years of McDonald's experience. I wasn't thinking about the customer service side of the business. I was only concentrating on fast food and flipping burgers.

Working at McDonald's taught me the skill of customer service. That know-how alone can launch your career and carry you through. Learning how to be a people person and honing in on others' needs to provide complete satisfaction is an art. Service with a smile will get you those relationship-building skills that everyone needs. Nobody wants to befriend a person who is always frowning. Smile. It changes how you and others feel too. Besides everyone is looking at your face. Practice your smile in the mirror until you find one you like.

To this day I still use the skills I developed at McDonald's. I utilize it in my cover letters when applying for opportunities, and I use it in my everyday life. The following is a sample of a portion of my cover letter using McDonald's:

I will provide your client base with the care in customer service and technical guidance through my years of experience in understanding the needs of every client. In each position I've held, I set the standard for customer satisfaction and training clients and employees by using skills that I began to develop in my teenage years of working at McDonald's, where customer satisfaction and service was a key element. There, I learned the importance of excellence in customer care and relationship building. Since then, I have made customer service and relationship building a driving factor in my technology career. Throughout my years in information technology, I have gained the ability to strengthen my service skills by keeping current with the ever-changing technology and sharpening interpersonal abilities through verbal and written communications. By doing so, I have established strong relationships and gained the respect of individuals across every organization I have worked for from c-level executives down the organizational chain.

That was just an example of how you will have to tap into past experiences and use them throughout your career. No experience is a wasted one. You just have to remember them and know when to use them.

One of my instructors told me, "You should always carry yourself accordingly. You never know who is watching or riding the train with you." And that is a valuable lesson right there. For example, an elevator can hold a lot of people, and you never know who is on it.

Fortunately one of my mentors, Mike Andrus, took me under his wing and taught me the ropes of building relationships.

Build associations, and offer your shared resources before asking others to assist you.

Some people give out their business cards to others only if it makes sense. I, on the other hand, give out my card to everyone I meet because it makes sense. If the person I meet does not have a good connection to do business together based on our lines of work, he or she, just as well as I, might know someone whom it does makes sense to do business with. In such cases, a warm introduction can take place to connect those individuals. And if you're lucky and make a deal, you just might get a referral fee sent your way. No card swap is ever a wasted exchange. Keep the term "one off" in mind when networking, another nugget from Mike Andrus. Each person is one off from your next introduction. It's a real thing that makes relationships work, sort of like the "six degrees of separation" concept.

My mom is a huge networker. She isn't afraid to approach anyone and ask any question. She has the power of influence and knows how to get what she wants. I learned how to approach people of high status from her. Her motto is, "If you don't ask, you'll never know."

In her many years in nursing, she's encountered and built relationships with wealthy people who took a liking to her. She cared for a few celebrities' relatives, such as the former head coach of the Philadelphia 76ers, the grandmother of one of Philadelphia's own rapper/actor, and a few others. She's also cared for some high-ranking officials and executives who were decision makers at some point in their careers.

Overall my mom has made some major connections and built relationships with many people by simply asking them a few questions without fear. I learned that art from her. I've had the opportunity to work directly with CEOs, COOs, federal regional directors, and many vice presidents of organizations.

And it's all because I learned the art of making connections and cultivating a relationship with them based on what I've learned from my mom.

I was having a conversation with a friend of mine in Dublin, Ireland, about communicating with upper management.

He said, "I need to learn how to effectively communicate with them."

I told him, "That's an easy task. Don't be afraid. It's as simple as that. That's one of the ways I learned to break the ice and communicate with CEOs and under. They want you to talk to them. When you do have a conversation with them, be honest. That's most critical. Use the right words, those that are effective and not harmful."

He laughed and said, "I don't want to brownnose."

I assured him, "its not brownnosing. It's building a relationship that is beneficial to both parties."

Take the time to speak to your upper management when passing in the hallways and strike up a conversation with them. Take a look at their LinkedIn profiles. You might learn that he or she is on a board or is associated with some organizations you are personally interested in. That can be your ice-breaking conversation.

And finally build relationships with multiple recruiters. You will need someone to keep you in the know of career opportunities from time to time. You will never know when you will need to make a career move, which can happen expectantly or not.

It's very important to have a few recruiters on speed dial. Touch base with them from time to time just to say hello. I don't care if you're looking for a job or not. Ask them to contact you occasionally with interesting positions that fit your background. Even if you're not looking for a new role, it's good to know what's out there. You just never know. The money just might be right to pull you out of your current position. Or the job could be closer to home. Or you might even find a work-from-home role, if that's up your alley.

Often recruiters will connect with you on LinkedIn just because they like your profile. Do yourself a favor and accept the connection request, and then send them a message to thank them for wanting to connect with you.

If a recruiter contacts you with a role and you're not looking to make a move, listen to what they have to say. It may or may not be a good fit for you. If not, let them know you will ask some of the people in your network if they have interest and pass along the information. You might luck out and receive a referral bonus. There's nothing like having a check come in the mail just for making a connection between two people you trust.

Never burn a bridge. Be kind to your network. You never know when you will need a helping hand.

CHAPTER 9
SPEAKING

Speak properly. Make sure you enunciate your words. Converse clearly and concisely. Always keep your head up when speaking and leave the slang at home.

I'm from Philadelphia, and we use the slang word "jawn," which can mean anything. If I am speaking with another Philadelphian and I use the term "jawn," that person will know exactly what I mean. Here's an example of a conversation between my best friend Brian and myself, both born and raised in Philly:

Brian asks, "Yo, Calv. Did you see those new jawns that just came out?"

I reply, "Yeah, B, those jawns are hot! I just picked up those jawns today, and they are comfortable!"

Brian asks, "Word! Which color did you get?"

I reply, "I grabbed the all-black jawns."

Brian says, "I was thinkin' 'bout scoopin' the black-and-white jawns."

What we really meant:
Brian asks, "Calvin, did you see the new sneakers that just came out?"

I reply, "Yes, Brian, those sneakers are really nice! I just purchased a pair today, and they are comfortable!"

Brian asks, "Really! What color did you get?"

I reply, "I selected the all-black pair."

Brian says, "I'm going to buy the black-and-white pair."

If you speak slang, you will need to know when to turn off that switch when speaking with people. There is a time and place for it, and it is not when you are conducting business. I don't care if you are conducting business with really good friends like Brian and I do.

When Brian and I have serious conversations, that street slang goes out the window. He and I grew up together since birth. Our level of comfort with each other is different from any other friendship I have. So if he and I can turn off that slang switch when conversing with each other, you too should know when to turn it off when having business conversations.

In 2014, I met with a young man from Detroit, and he asked if I were from Philadelphia. I had multiple people tell me that they could not tell I was from Philadelphia because I spoke properly. I take that as a compliment because I've worked hard to know when and where to turn that switch on and off. I recently started correcting myself from saying "wooder" to saying "water," as we say it in Philly.

I told him, "Born and raised!"

He said, "I can't hear your Philly accent like I've heard in other people from the city."

I told him, "I know how to turn it off and on. There was a time and place for it."

Since he and I were meeting for me to possibly mentor him, I needed to turn off my Philly. I had to represent myself as best as possible. It would be difficult for me to take career advice from someone who doesn't speak proper English. I'm not saying he or she wouldn't have anything to offer me. I am saying that my focus wouldn't be on the advice. It would be on his or her enunciation and choice of words (or lack thereof).

Pay close attention to your speech as well as others. I have a colleague named Tristan Nunnally, a Temple University alumni. From the day I met him in October 2012, he caught my attention with his speech. Tristan pronounces his words properly and with conviction.

One day I told Tristan, "I admired the way you speak."

He asked, "Really?" and was shocked.

"I said, "You speak clearly and concisely and how you pronounce words caught my attention from the day we met.

I also told him, "I wish I spoke like him."

He said, "I don't think there is anything special about how I speak."

I assured him, "there is."

As of August 17, 2014, I haven't attended college. I attended a technical trade school that only offered one course on speaking, Business Communications. Outside of that, I studied the communication styles of people who caught my attention. I knew from the home training my parents gave me on how to turn the switch on and off when conducting business and having serious conversations. No one wants to hear improper English when communicating in a professional setting.

When speaking with an individual, keep eye contact with him or her. If talking with more than one person, rotate among the people to let them know you are speaking with all of them and not just one person. If you are presenting to a crowd, scan over your audience and engage them. No one wants to be in the presence of a speaker who is looking down all the time.

If you are presenting, it is a given to glance down at your notes to ensure you are on track. But when delivering your message, you must know your material so you don't have to constantly look down and read from your notes. You want to keep the attention of your audience by engaging them as you speak. Don't lock into one person. Connect with as many people as possible. You don't want to give your eye contact to two or three people in a room of three thousand.

I've been in presentations when the speaker would lock in on a few individuals. It can be distracting to the audience. People may begin to wonder what is so special about those sole individuals who keep getting the looks from the speaker. Once that happens, the speaker has lost some of his or her audience's attention, and his or her message is not received.

You will not be able to make eye contact with everyone in the room. But you can scan over the space as you speak. Try not to be an oscillating fan with your head and neck. Engage different areas as you're speaking throughout your presentation.

The first time I had to present to an audience was when I was in Ms. Coleman's fourth-grade class. I'll never forget it. We had to memorize and recite poems in front of the class. When that day came, I could have crapped my pants. There was no way I was going to stand up in front of a class full of my peers and recite a poem. Ms. Coleman asked for volunteers to go first. The classroom full of ambitious students started raising their hands. Guess whose hand never went up? Mine! I was hoping she wouldn't notice I didn't go up to recite.

The time came. I was the penultimate student to go. So of course Ms. Coleman chose me to go instead of John. I took my time peeling myself out of my desk and walked slowly to the front of the class. I stood there looking out onto the audience, and I did not blink. I was frozen. All eyes were on me. It felt like my classmates' eyes were lasers just burning through me.

I wanted to run out of the class and never come back. Then the bell rang to go out for recess. I was saved. I had that one last hope that Ms. Coleman would forget that I didn't recite the poem and move on with the lesson plan.

That wasn't the case. We came back from recess, and it was on again. Calvin had to go to the front of the class to recite his poem. Then my classmate John, who was last, said he would recite it with me since I was nervous. So we recited the poem together, and I felt a little relaxed knowing I wasn't alone.

At that age, I had no idea what an introvert was. I just knew I didn't like being the center of attention; nor did I like speaking in front of crowds. I had my subset of friends who I was comfortable with, and that was all. I wasn't used to change. Now I embrace it!

I have a tip for my fellow introverts. If you're nervous when presenting to an audience and you want to look out into the crowd, gaze past them by keeping your attention on the tops of their heads. It will appear as if you are observing the people behind them. This will eliminate you from giving direct eye contact to the crowd.

If you haven't taken any formal courses that would have taught you how to communicate, look into Toastmasters International, a communications and leadership development group that helps individuals become better speakers and leaders. They have clubs that meet a few times a month in various locations all over the world.

I attended a Toastmasters meeting once, and I thought it was a great forum where people from various backgrounds came together to help each other succeed in the area of communication. Each person had to bring his or her speech and present it to the group. Once completed, the group would critique each person's speech and point out the mistakes to assist the person in becoming a better speaker. An exercise called Table Topics helped each person make an impromptu speech.

To me, this is a great group to be a part of. But the introvert wouldn't allow me to speak up and become a member. I plan to join a club in the near future simply because I feel the need to sharpen my communication skills. My mimic and studying of individuals will only take me so far. I also plan to enroll in a university to obtain my bachelor's and master's degree. (I am not sure if I want to remain in IT or transition to some area of business.)

Hopefully by the time you are reading this book, my LinkedIn profile will be updated with my education reflecting that I've enrolled in a university. And with any luck, I've gotten out of my own way as an introvert and became a member of Toastmasters International.

In 2005 or 2006, I learned to step outside of my comfort zones and forced myself to be more aggressive and join groups. I became a member of various networking groups, which helped me learn more communication styles and forced me to acquire the ability how to introduce myself. I learned how to

- give a thirty-second pitch about who I am and what I do for a living,
- speak with passion about the things I'm most excited about, and
- speak with confidence and conviction.

I also learned I need to study my material, just in case someone asks me specific questions about my associations.

Consider it to be like your résumé. You should know what you've done.

Learn how to be a well-spoken person. People will always remember one of two things about you: if you're good or bad at something. It's better to be remembered as good than bad. So whatever you do, be a good one.

In 1997, I heard Will Smith, one of my role models, give an acceptance speech when he won a Video Music Award. I admired his ability to go after his dreams with making music and becoming a world-renowned actor. But during his speech, it seemed like every other word was preceded with "umm." My thoughts went crazy. I was thinking, *How could a rapper/actor not know how to speak without using 'umm'?* He puts words together when creating rhymes, and he memorizes scripts for television and movies. When I witnessed this, I had to—and still make a conscious effort to—watch how often I saw "umm" when I'm speaking. It just doesn't sound good.

Over the years Will Smith's acceptance speeches have gotten better, and he no longer says "umm." He took the time to learn how to focus on his delivery and eliminated the filler words. Will Smith gets straight to the point and always has a great message for people to walk away with a few takeaways.

Once you have some time, look up Will Smith's acceptance speeches on YouTube. You'll see what I'm talking about, and you'll observe his progress over the years in his speeches. You might also learn a few things as well.

CHAPTER 10
DIVERSITY

Embrace diversity because it is all around you. As you know, you will interact with many people from different walks of life. You will intermingle with people of different races, sexes, and sexual preferences. You will meet racists. You will encounter people with different spiritual or political beliefs. You will converse with vegetarians and meat eaters. You will talk to playful and serious people. You will interact with hard workers and slackers. Then there will be the people with body odors and those who wear too much cologne or perfume.

When interacting with people, you have to treat all with respect, whether you agree with their personal choices in life or not. It is critical to remain neutral and not express your preferences. Even if someone asks you for your opinion on matters outside of work, it is your job to govern yourself and not engage in such conversations. Your opinion could offend the person you are talking to and furthermore upset someone in earshot of the conversation.

My dad always told me to never talk politics and religion at work. That is so true! I've witnessed a heated debate in a former company where I worked when religious beliefs began to come up in conversation. My two colleagues began spouting off about who God is and which messenger was the truest. I kindly removed myself from the area because I did not want to engage or even be associated with that conversation. All it would take was for someone to walk by, hear the topic, and see who was there, and we would all have been guilty by association even if we did not take part in it. So I left the scene and found another place to work temporarily.

Thus far in my career, I've experienced a lot of diversity. One company I worked for had an individual who had a sex change. HR sent out a message to the entire organization explaining the matter. It was very touchy, and Legal was involved as well.

They explained that John Doe was having a sex change and said how he was going to go through a transition over the next few months. We were informed that John was taking hormone pills and body parts would begin to appear. We were instructed to not stare or gossip about it. If we did, we would lose our jobs immediately.

As time went on, John's hair began to grow longer, and breasts began to develop. Soon after, HR sent out another message to the organization, stating that John would begin to use the women's restroom. And not much longer after that, another message came out stating that John's transition had been completed, and we were now to address him as Jane.

During that entire process, I did not see Jane until a few weeks after she returned to work. Once I did see her in passing, I had to do my best not to stare or make her feel uncomfortable. I spoke. She talked, and my thoughts went crazy. I remained calm and collected because this was a human being who made a decision and chose to live a way she knew was best for her. I respected that decision and moved on. Certain things you hear and think you will never experience. But if you do, you must respect others' decisions and treat them how you would want to be treated.

Another organization I worked for made it mandatory for every employee to take diversity training yearly. This was right up my alley, simply because I had experienced quite a few diverse situations in my career at that point. I wanted to make sure I handled them properly.

So some diversity consultants came in to train us. One of the first things they spoke about was knowing your audience. To the average person, your audience is the person you are talking to. We stood corrected. Your audience is the people who can hear you, whether they are in front of you, in an office or cubicle, or just passing by. Whoever can hear you speaking can hold you responsible for anything and everything you say. And just because you may not be speaking to that person, you could offend him or her with your conversation topic, and he or she has every right to report you to HR. If reported, you could be reprimanded with a warning, suspension, and/or termination.

Some words of wisdom include keeping your opinions and personal conversations for places outside of the workplace. Also be aware that work-hosted events are still considered to be in the workplace, whether they are in the employer's physical building or not. If your organization hosts an after-work event, you are considered to still be at work.

Another company I worked for hired several people who were a part of the gay and lesbian community, along with their partners. Some employees did not care for it too much and thought they were being passed over for those job opportunities they never applied for and wouldn't apply for. They felt preferential treatment was given to the partners of the current employees.

At times some opinions were being thrown out there about it, some very loud and obnoxious. Others were quiet whispers amongst colleagues. For someone like me who doesn't care about anyone's sexual preference, it became bothersome. I didn't think it was right for those individuals to express themselves so loudly and in the workplace.

It could have brought on tension and possibly made those affected feel intimidated and fearful to come to work. It is critical to consider everyone's feelings and to live by a simple rule taught to most people in preschool, "Treat others how you want to be treated, regardless of their backgrounds."

For example, on this employee's first day, a colleague approached him. "Hey, do you want some beef?"

The new employee responded, "No, thank you. I don't eat meat."

The colleague yelled, "Why do we keep hiring these people?"

I immediately jumped up. "You cannot say that! His lifestyle has nothing to do with you. And you need to respect that!"

The colleague said, "I was just joking and only referring to people who didn't eat meat."

I further explained, "Our new employee might not have known you were joking and could have been highly offended. This is his first day. He doesn't know you or your style of joking, let alone anyone else that might have been in earshot of your comments."

That was a lawsuit waiting to happen.

There are many diversity courses available to enroll in. I suggest you find one or two and sign up just for personal education. The last thing you want to do is offend someone. So it is best to arm yourself with the knowledge on how not to insult anyone in the workplace and life in general.

We all must coexist in this world. It is best to know how to get along with one another in every area of life. If your organization does not offer courses in diversity, maybe you should suggest they look into it.

Employers should not assume everyone knows better. It would be nice if we all did. The truth of the matter is that we don't. We may not know how to deal with a diversity issue that is brought against us. The training should teach you how to handle them if faced with it. It is education on what to do and not do if faced with a situation.

Cook Ross, Inc. provides a host of diversity tools that you as an individual can purchase. One in particular is the Cultural Communication Guide (http://www.cookross.com). I purchased this guide a few years ago just to give myself an idea on how to communicate with different cultures. You can even introduce this site to your organization if you feel it would help with diversity within your workplace.

CHAPTER 11
WORK-RELATED TRAVEL

When traveling for work, remember that it's a privilege, not always a requirement. From the very moment you leave your home, you are on work hours. Whether you are traveling to arrive the night before or the same business day, you are representing your company. With that in mind, dress in business attire. I'm not saying you should suit up. I'm simply telling you to dress the same way you would if you were going to work. If your culture requires a tie, wear one. If you travel at night, I would think going tieless is acceptable.

I tend to dress a bit more businesslike because I never know whom I will meet. Your current position is more than likely not your final role. If you're not on the market looking for a new position, the opportunity can always present itself. If it does, you want to look the part. I call it "ready set go" mode.

Know your limits. If you are visiting a satellite office, client, or partner, you need to know your boundaries with your food intake if you are being treated to lunch or dinner. You also need to know your alcohol limits. If you know you can drink with the best of them, don't. It's probably best to not drink at all. You don't want to be labeled as greedy or an alcoholic. Follow the lead of your supervisor, if he or she is with you. If you are with clients, try to refrain from drinking. If it's casual, have a drink if they are. Keep the mind-set that someone is always judging you, so be careful.

You also need to know the spending limit if you possess a corporate credit card. Do not exceed your per diem (an allowance given to you by your organization for specific daily needs while traveling on business, i.e. for certain meals). If you want something extra, purchase it out of your own pocket. You are responsible for the credit card you have been entrusted with. So be responsible.

If your travel is for multiple days, pack an extra business outfit just in case something happens to one of the outfits you packed. The last thing you want to do is scramble, trying to figure out where you can purchase clothes. There is nothing wrong with over packing and being prepared for a possible accident like a hotel iron burning your shirt or staining your pants. It is possible, so why not be prepared?

When ironing your clothes with a hotel iron and board, first check the iron to see if there are stains and melted material on the bottom. If it is, call the front desk and ask for another iron to be brought up to your room. You don't want to begin ironing your clothes and have the iron ruin them. Also check the board. If the board looks dirty, request another one.

There is such a thing as business traveling etiquette. If you don't know it, look it up online. If you Google *business travel etiquette* tips, you will find a host of sites that provide tips.

If traveling abroad, research the culture of the country you are visiting. Learn their mannerisms. Research how to address someone when saying hello and good-bye. Find out if he or she shakes hands when greeting. Also look up how to properly hand your business card to them. Also be cognizant of your tone when talking. If you have an aggressive delivery, practice toning it down.

If your company does not offer such trainings, do yourself a favor and research the culture yourself. It will benefit you for future engagements and traveling opportunities, whether for business or pleasure. Learning about different cultures and acting accordingly will show your hosts you respect their way of life and you took the time to learn.

CHAPTER 12
STUDY YOUR ENVIRONMENT

In *Audacity of Hope: Reclaiming the American Dream* by President Barack Obama, President George W. Bush offered some advice to the young senator,

> You've got a bright future, very bright. I've been in this town a long time and it can be tough. When you get a lot of attention like you've been getting people start gunning for you. And it won't necessarily be just coming from my side you understand—from yours too. Everybody will be waiting for you to slip. So watch yourself (2006).

Imagine that. A Republican president was giving a young Democratic senator words of wisdom to help him along in his career. I'm sure that golden nugget President George W. Bush gave to Senator Barack Obama helped him study his environment more than he probably was. In simpler terms, President Bush told Senator Obama to watch his own back because the people you think are on your side aren't always playing fair and have their own agendas in mind.

This doesn't mean you need to change your mission. It simply means to stay the course you charted for yourself. You may have to do a few things different to get the same results you are seeking. But at least you will be prepared.

At the beginning stages of your career, you pretty much know what direction you want to head in. Everyone starts out as entry level. Then you work your way up by gaining experience, proving you are capable and making the right connections and decisions.

Now you have some form of navigational system that is guiding you, whether it's you watching someone's steps who is in the position you want or a mentor giving you advice about your next career move. Or your organization is paying attention to your career path, and they offer you advancement opportunities that will further your career.

You must study your environment. Sometimes this means seeing the direction before it has been voiced. This will allow you to get in position for a transition.

CHAPTER 13
DESIRE

When I was in a technical trade school in 1995, I had a business communications class. We had a special guest come speak to our class one day. His presence was like the signature statement of celebrity chef Emeril Lagasse ("Bam!") from the time he walked into the door and went through this entire presentation. His name is Mike Andrus. Yes, my mentor.

Back then, Mike was running his business, Andrus Associates, an IT consulting firm. He spoke to our class about being a business owner, conducting business, building relationships, and starting our careers. I was nineteen years old then. Mike's presentation made such an impression on me to the point where I wanted to work for him. I said this aloud and released it into the universe for it to grab hold of it. They say, "If you want something, you have to speak it into existence." I didn't know much about that back then. But I do now.

Within a few months, I was set to graduate from the trade school and embark on my career. I didn't have much luck finding jobs due to a lack of experience. I had also forgotten about Mike Andrus. One day I spoke to Career Services from the trade school, asking for assistance in finding a job. I had my résumé reviewed, and within a week or two, I received a phone call from Mike Andrus, offering me a job with his firm.

At the time of the call, I was working at McDonald's. So my dad called me, giving me the good news of landing a job. I was to start the next day, having to drive to Raritan, New Jersey, three hours away, to head up to Johnson & Johnson as a contracted IT professional. Little did I know that my desire from hearing Mike Andrus's presentation and releasing my desire to work for him into the universe would come to pass!

To this day, Mike and I are really good friends. He has helped me along the way in my career with giving me my first opportunity at Johnson & Johnson, along with numerous opportunities and experiences to help grow me as a professional and individual. And to him I am very grateful for that.

If something is meant for you to have and you have the desire and will to put it out there in prayer, it will come to pass as long as you believe and work toward that goal. That was one of the many blessings I've received in my life thus far.

I've had plenty of desires, and I worked smart to receive them. It takes effort on your part. Having a desire and not putting in work to receive it is like having all the money in the world but never buying anything to enjoy it.

Put it out there. Work your spiritually designed system that God has given you access to. Pray and be a blessing to others who need a helping hand, whether you offer words of wisdom, make a connection for others, or even offer a monetary gift to someone in need. Extending good deeds into the universe for others opens the floodgates of blessings for you.

Everyone has desires, hopes, and dreams. When it comes to your career, most people see themselves doing what they envisioned as their ideal job. Oftentimes it's doing something you love, something that gets your juices bubbling or whatever your core meaningful purpose in life is. This dream position is something you desire, hope, and dream for.

With that being said, this is where your career path has led you, in your dreams, that is, because you haven't gotten there yet. What you are seeing is in your head and heart as the place you feel you are meant to be. It's all in your dreams. You either haven't embarked on your career or you are in a meaningless job that just gets you experience or is the place you decided to be in for the time being to get you by.

In the mid-1980s, we lived very close to the Philadelphia international airport. When my friends and I would play basketball, one of my best friends would always get distracted while on the basketball court. Anytime an airplane would fly over us, he would stop and just look up in the sky.

We would say, "Nae, pay attention and play ball!"

Nae told us back then, "Yo, I'm going to be a pilot one day."

Nae had a desire to fly airplanes. When we graduated high school, Nae left Philadelphia and moved to Newark, Delaware, to attend Wilmington College. He also attended flight school to become a pilot.

As the years passed by, Nae and I would talk. And he would tell me how he was involved in flight competitions in Florida. All I could do was be proud for Nae. He was living out his dream. A few more years passed by, and Nae was a certified pilot. He began flying for a major airline. He then received numerous promotions, and now he is an international pilot.

One day in the winter of 2014, a few friends of ours got together and went to visit Nae. We shared lots of laughs and reminisced on stories from our childhood. We began talking about all of our Instagram posts, and then a serious moment struck us. We started talking about how Nae posts pictures from his travels across the world.

Nae stopped and said, "This is for y'all. I post these pictures so y'all can see the world just like I am."

That's my homie right there! That's all love. Not everyone will be able to visit other countries. So Nae thinks of us and posts his journeys so we can share his experiences.

All it takes is having a dream, the desire, and the passion to be brave enough to go for what you know you want. One of my best friends, Napoleon Brown, a kid from Southwest Philly, is representing for anyone who wants it bad enough to just go do it.

Understand this: you have to create your own career path. You have to chart out your directions and follow them. In today's standards, companies do not draw up career paths. It is very rare to find an organization that will hire you for a position and tell you, "Two to three years from now, we will promote you from level one to level two. And in another two to three years, we will promote you to level three and so on and so forth."

Today it is your job to chart out your own career path. Most companies will keep you in the same position year after year if you are doing a great job at it. Their thoughts are, "Why should we move this person to the next level if he or she hasn't asked to be moved and/or if he or she is doing such a great job in his or her current position?"

The company may throw you a few increases in your salary over time, but that may end up being all you get. If you're lucky, you might get some type of meaningless new title just to keep your mouth shut. You have to first know what you want and then go for it. You must show the desire and action that you want more.

It is your job to know where you want to go as a person, an employee, and business owner. If you know what makes your core being thrive with ambition, do that. If you know where you want to go within an organization, chart your path. If you own your own business and you see your business growing further than you thought it would, you must keep going.

As an employee, it is your job to study the business, see the direction it is going, and visualize where you fit in during that growth. Figure out what you can do to help the business grow. Not only does helping the business grow help the business, it assists you as well. Once you have a definite plan in place, have a conversation with your direct supervisor. Tell him or her, "I've done my research on how the company is growing, and I would like opportunities to help the company move forward with its plan. And this is how I would like to do that."

I had a colleague at MaaS360 by Fiberlink who saw the company's direction. He studied the product to gain as much knowledge as he could. Not only did he make himself more knowledgeable of the product, he did that because he had a bigger desire in his mind to not stay in the same position he was hired to do. He knew demonstrating MaaS360 was not his last stop. He had a desire to travel to customer sites and demo the product with various sales representatives within the organization. He showed ambition, knowledge, and the will to go further than his job description described. With that, he drew out his plan and presented it to our director.

He basically told her, "This is what I am doing. This is where I see the company going, and this is what I want to do to help the company get there."

He had a meeting with our director and told her what his desires were to help the company grow. The part you might not see is that he didn't solely do it for the company. He did it more so for himself.

You are building your résumé. You are creating stories to tell when meeting other businesspeople and making connections. You are making a name for yourself as you mold yourself into the person your desire to be within your career.

I really look forward to hearing about and seeing Matthew Shaver's career growth. Matt is genuinely a very nice guy. He is always willing to assist in areas within his own expertise as well as outside of it. If you ever meet him, you will see that in your first conversation with him. Check him out on LinkedIn. His profile is pretty cool.

On the other side of the coin, you have the person who wants and desires certain things within his or her career but does nothing to get those things except complain about being looked over. If you don't want to be looked over or forgotten about, you have to make yourself known. You have to go further than you might not be willing to go.

Napoleon Hill talks about that in *Three Feet from Gold*. You're almost there but not quite. Then you make the decision to stop and quit just when you were a few feet from your heart's desire.

If you're not willing to work harder for yourself, no one will be willing to give you anything but the bare minimum. And why should they give you more when you only give yourself that? Ask yourself that question a few times. And email me your answers to polishedthebook@gmail.com. I'm interested in hearing what you have to say if this is your reality.

One thing I've learned about life is that it only gives you what you put out, nothing more and nothing less. Chart your course for your career. It will be the best thing you could ever do for your calling.

CHAPTER 14
FOCUS

Meditate on what you want to accomplish. Write down your ideas so you can have a visual plan to draw from. If you're a spiritual person, pray about it. Ask God to give you the tools needed to give you your heart's desire. I start from prayer when I need to focus on accomplishing a goal. I tell God my desires, and I ask Him to give me the tools needed to accomplish my objectives.

I worked for the National Park Service as an IT contractor for almost ten years. I knew at some point that I needed to leave there and get back into the private sector. I knew the people who renewed my contract would be retiring soon, and there was no guarantee the next group of individuals would be willing to renew my contract. So I made the decision that it was time to move on. I prayed to God and asked for the direction I needed to make my move. I told God what I wanted.

- I wanted a job in Center City Philadelphia, making the amount of money God saw fit for me to make.
- I wanted to work for an organization that had opportunities to advance.
- I wanted to be in a company that was not going to fold in ten years.
- I wanted to work for a company with free parking.

You get the picture. I told God exactly what I wanted. So I began looking into various organizations: Gartner and GSI Commerce, now eBay and Fiberlink. I looked into Gartner because IT research will never die out. GSI Commerce was on my radar because e-commerce will always exist with the advancements of technology; I researched Fiberlink because the use of mobile devices will do nothing but advance.

I've been around the block a few times within some of the organizations I've worked for. At the time I was a part of two acquisitions. My first was First Union National Bank acquiring CoreStates National Bank in November 1997, just about three days after I started working there. Then I experienced another acquisition when I worked for Zeneca Pharmaceuticals during their merger with Astra Pharmaceuticals in 1999. I didn't want to experience another acquisition and possibly become a displaced employee. That was one thing I left out of my prayers when I was telling God my desires for another career opportunity. It is very important to be specific when praying for your heart's desires.

Then again there's a reason for everything. Not mentioning an acquisition turned out to be a great thing in my favor. I received a promotion due to acquisition this time around. In turn God gave me some instructions to leave certain people alone because they meant no good to me and I to them. God instructed me to pray every day and prepare my résumé in such a way that focused on my success and key projects. Then I updated my LinkedIn profile. After those two pieces were intact, I began to look for opportunities.

God told me I was looking too far. "Why are you looking in every direction except right in front of you?" I wasn't too sure what that meant, but I stopped looking in every direction and started observing in front of me. A product we used at the National Park Service was called MaaS360 MDM (Mobile Device Management). Yes, MaaS360 by Fiberlink. This was before they became an IBM company.

So I looked right in front of me, went to the MaaS360 website, and started monitoring it for job opportunities. I found a position, prayed about it, applied for the job, went on a few interviews, and continued to pray on it. Then I went on a few more interviews for this position and prayed some more. Then I accepted the offer.

I took the time to focus on what I wanted, and I got it. Not only did I apply this type of focus on my career, I use this in every area of my life. Take the time to understand what is of your heart and mind. Write notes to yourself when you begin to brainstorm about a change so you don't forget it.

In today's age of technology, we have many tools at our fingertips. There are no excuses for not having pen and paper. Use your smartphone, tablet, or computer to write down your thoughts. Don't try to remember these things to jot down later. Chances are, you will forget.

When I'm driving and a thought comes to me, I'll pull over and write it down, or I'll use the voice recorder app on my phone. If I'm in the middle of a conversation, I will excuse myself for a moment to write down that thought. Of course it depends on whom I'm speaking with. Another thing I learned is to tell the person that I want to write down a note to myself about this conversation so I don't forget. I've gotten some kudos from people for doing that. Just as fast as your thoughts come, they will go even faster.

If you think you will remember your thoughts, please take my advice. Use your technology to write it out. I thought I would remember many times, and my memory has failed me almost every time. Another trick I often use is texting myself once something comes to mind. We have so many options at our fingertips. We need to use them.

Two of my former colleagues, Jeremy and Josh, came up with a plan to develop a training program for MaaS360's partners that was designed to help the resellers understand the product. Because Jeremy and Josh took the time to focus on a solution to help the company and its partners understand our solution, Chris Clark, president of MaaS360 by Fiberlink, recognized them with the Innovator's Award. It also came with a monetary gift.

Not all companies recognize employees who come up with ideas to help the organization. If your employer does not award you with awards or gifts for your efforts, don't let that stop you from focusing on something you want to accomplish. Incentives such as monetary gifts always help, but don't let that be your driving force to be innovative. Be groundbreaking because it is in you to be. At least you will walk away with the experience it takes to complete a project and, even better, a story to tell and a résumé builder.

There are three Fs you need to be aware of: family, friends, and foes. There will be people in your life who will try to distract you from your goals. Recognize them before it's too late. They will see you focusing on your tasks and try to lure you away with temptations they know you like.

Be strong and don't fall for it. The smallest distraction can set you back from completing your projects. Sad to say, but think of them as the devil sitting on your left shoulder, like in the cartoons, trying to tempt you to do things you know are not right and are sinful. People will use things like sex, money, food, and other extracurricular activities they know you enjoy to pull you away. You don't want to allow these things to happen and make you feel like you wasted your time doing those things by allowing someone to pull you away.

I'm not saying to not have fun during your time working to accomplish your goals. We all need balance and downtime to regroup. But I'm telling you to not let it happen during your working time. You are in control of your downtime. You control your clock. You determine when your free time will be. If your family, friends, and foes cannot respect that, say, "Oh, well!" and find new people to enjoy your downtime with if you need people at all. It sounds cold, but just remember that you have goals you need to focus on accomplishing. Don't be afraid to tell people no. When you need to focus on your objectives, the word "no" will be your best friend.

People sometimes genuinely forget what you have going on and will ask you to do things with them or for them. Telling them no and reminding them what you are working on will help jog their memory that you are focusing on a project that you must complete.

CHAPTER 15
PLAYING THE GAME

In *Mandela's Way: Lesson on Life, Love and Courage* by Richard Stengel, Nelson Mandela said, "If you want to play the part, you have to wear the right costume" (2010). This is my personal opinion, and it's based on experiences and observations throughout my years in the workforce and interactions with others. Being an African American male, I know what it means to have to wear the right costume to fit into the right part. In order to really become successful in a corporate environment, we have to fit into a certain mold. This isn't true for every African American. Some are accepted as they depend on their upbringing and educational backgrounds.

I've seen some African Americans who were raised in the suburbs and attended some predominantly white schools and prestigious universities not have to worry about changing who they are to be accepted. I've also seen those who come from that same background try their best to fit into the mold of an inner-city black kid and just not cut it. So it goes both ways.

Take me as an example, a black kid raised in a broken home, running back and forth between my mom's and dad's houses. I went from Southwest Philly to West Philly and back, packing bags for the weekend and sometimes taking all of my clothes to live full time with one parent from time to time.

My education was from the Philadelphia Public School District in the years of 1981 to 1994, including my year to repeat the sixth grade. I graduated from John Bartram High School and attended a technical trade school known back then as Computer Learning Center. I had an opportunity to attend Drexel University, but I felt I wasn't mature enough to handle the college lifestyle. So trade school it was.

I had the inner workings of a straight-up city kid with how to get by the next day on my mind at all times. My parents both worked in great professions, my mom in nursing and my dad in graphic design. They made ends meet. They also hustled their butts off by working side jobs, my mom in private duty nursing and my dad in freelance graphics. Watching my parents hustle every day made me learn that same trait. They did their best in giving me great examples on how to survive and how not to live if I didn't want to be without.

I've seen my parents act one way at home around family and friends and another way when it came to business. One day my dad took me on a run, and in the car he said, "I'm going to show you how to conduct yourself when it comes to taking care of business."

We went into an insurance company so he could get car insurance. My dad started speaking more properly than he already does. He was doing a lot of smiling, and he kept eye contact with the agent. Once it was all over, he shook the agent's hand and said, "Thank you. It was nice doing business with you."

Polished

Once we left the office, my dad said, "When you become an adult, anytime you need to conduct business, that's how you do it. You cannot speak with people in a manner you would speak with your family and friends. You have to talk properly. You have to enunciate with confidence. You have to keep eye contact and give a firm handshake before and after the business meeting." That was my first encounter of playing the game and wearing the right costume.

I had no idea that life lesson my dad gave me that day would have such a great impact on my life and career. I can honestly say that who I am when conducting business in a corporate setting or in any personal business environment is not who I am when I am around my family and friends. It's just a costume because I am playing a part for those moments.

In my opinion, my white colleagues don't seem to have to play that role of wearing a costume. They come to work being who they are. Now I don't want to come off as sounding angry or bitter because I am far from that. I'm simply speaking about my observations.

One example I encountered was in 1996. I was working for a computer reseller and distribution center as a team lead configuration specialist. There were very few African Americans as configuration specialists, but once we got together and stood around for a brief conversation, the managers would come over and break it up by saying, "What's going on here is a posse forming. Let's get back to work."

But once our white colleagues would get together to talk about last night's baseball or hockey game, the managers would join in, laugh and joke, and sometimes even have debates on the games. But we (the black guys) couldn't have a few minutes to stand around and talk about basketball or football for a few minutes.

There are differences in who and what is accepted. I did a little test. One night I watched a hockey game, went to work the next day, and struck up a conversation with the group of black guys about it. I wanted to see if the manager would come over and join the conversation. He came over, but he didn't join the conversation. He told us to get back to work but then joined the white guys' conversation about the game.

The second test involved me watching another hockey game, but I struck up a conversation with our white colleagues to see if the manager would come over and tell me to leave or join in. He joined in. I found it funny because I was speaking properly and I was accepted into the group that day. I wore a different costume in order to be accepted. It's kind of messed up if you think about it, but it's true.

The quote at the beginning of this chapter by the late Nelson Mandela is a reality for many people regardless of their nationality. I can only speak from my personal experiences. I've seen many individuals from many nationalities have to wear costumes in order to get where they want to be in a business profession.

Think about people with language barriers and accents. They have to work extra hard in order to be heard properly. When they speak to others about business or general conversation, the listener sometimes asks them to repeat themselves. They sometimes get frustrated and become rude to the speaker by making inappropriate remarks based on their pronunciation of words.

It's not easy being a minority for anyone. Try going to another country where their first language is not yours. Try having to adjust to a culture that is not where you came from or your upbringing. Adjusting to anything new takes time. If you want others to be patient with you, you must first have tolerance. For me, it goes back to my parents teaching me to have respect for others, regardless if they give you deference in return. It may not feel good at the time, but you will have a few things happen:

1. You know you did the right thing by giving respect.
2. Those people who did not return the respect to you will think back on the moment they were rude to you, and it just might open a soft spot in their hearts.
3. You've distributed good karma for yourself out into the universe to be returned to you at some point in your life.

Here is a quote I enjoy, "Find you and be that." I'm not sure who was the first to ever say it, but it makes total sense. It takes time and self-observation to find out who you truly are, what you truly enjoy, and what you truly want for your life. We must find out what we are most passionate about. Once we do, that's when we have found ourselves. Then we can be that. It causes an effortless feeling once we add our contribution to the universe. Give back what was given to you as a gift to others.

Wearing the right costume doesn't always require you losing yourself to get to where you want to be in life. We all have to make a living by doing something. Sometimes that something requires a costume to become accomplished. And once things change in your life—and they will because no path is straight—you might have to change into a different costume to fit the occasion.

CHAPTER 16
SPIRITUALITY

My spiritual beliefs don't allow me to judge anyone's actions, beliefs, decisions, or religion. I am of God, and I want nothing but the best for others and myself. I am not going to preach a sermon in this chapter. I am merely going to tell you that it is important to believe in some form of spiritual force in a positive manner. My upbringing is Christianity. Both of my parents are Christians. Once I became of age to make my own decisions, I wanted to explore other religions. I looked into Islam and Buddhism mostly.

I gravitated to Buddhism because it sits well with my spirit. I am a Christian. I believe we all speak to one God, just through different messengers. I pray every morning through Jesus Christ and throughout the day. I also practice awareness and mindfulness. I receive guidance through the Holy Spirit. God gives me directions to follow. No, I don't always follow them. But when I do follow them to a T, I never fail.

Spirituality is in everything you fashion your life around. It's your everyday inner workings of the world. It's how you think, act, and live and your decision-making. It is important to have a positive spirit as positivity brings good things into your life. Positive thoughts result into positive actions and positive receipts from others in your life. It's a universal law called the law of attraction.

It's important to have a positive spiritual connection with God. He is in all of us, and God wants us to accept the way of the light. However you choose, choose life. Choose love and kindness.

On March 17, 2015, God spoke to me and told me to let it go because I didn't understand it. I knew exactly what God was talking about. So I dropped Buddhism. I wrote it in my journal to make it real and to give it life. My journal entry reads, "I had to let go of something I didn't fully understand. After I let it go, I felt a release on my soul; heaviness lifted."

Then God said to me, "Well done, son. Now I can bless you."

I can honestly say I was looking for a fix for my life that already exists within me. That's the full understanding that God is all I ever need. God puts a calling on all of our lives from the time we are conceived. It's up to us to answer that call when we hear it from Him once we are on earth. That calling is the gifts He gives us. Those presents are not for us to keep. They are for us to give and share with others here on earth. One of my gifts is this book. I'm sharing my experiences with you because God gave me the talent of writing and expressing myself through this medium.

To me, spirituality is like your drive (your hustle). You get what you give. If you give a lot of positive, you'll receive a lot in return. If you give a lot of negative, you'll receive a lot back. The universe operates on the seeds—good or bad—that are planted. So of course your harvest depends on the type of seeds you've planted.

I'm not sure what your spiritual beliefs are, and I'm not trying to make you believe what I do. I am trying to use my beliefs and #payitforward in hopes that the message I am sharing helps you along the way. I'm also hoping it gives you life and energy to pay it forward to others who are working toward making their mark on this earth.

As promised, I'm not going to preach a sermon. But I do pray this helps you along with your positive journey throughout your life and career.

CHAPTER 17
SELF: MY NOTES TO YOU

You Cannot Give Up on Yourself!

- Be sure to take time for yourself every day. Choose the best time for yourself once you feel you are most receptive in a space where you feel positive energy. Whether it's in a space in your home, in a park, or on a walk—wherever you are at peace and of clear mind—that's where you want to take time for yourself. Be sure to rest properly as much as you can. There will be days that your rest time will be compromised because your schedule is changing throughout the week. If you attend events for personal or professional growth, times will come when your bedtime changes. As a word of advice, if you go to bed later than normal, make it a point not to be late to work or an appointment the next day. No one wants to hear about your late night from

the night before. Everyone's time is valuable and should not be wasted.
- Set your alarm clock before you leave the house that morning to be sure you do not forget to do so when you arrive home that night. Also set your alarm on your smartphone as a backup. And to take it a step further, ask a friend to give you a call just to be sure you are up and at it.
- Don't take fish to work for lunch. It will smell up the office after you microwave it. That bad odor is along the lines of the stench of burnt microwave popcorn throughout the office.
- Set your phone notifications to vibrate while in the office. Nothing is more annoying than hearing someone's notifications constantly going off.
- Post a proper picture on your LinkedIn profile. If you can afford it, get a professional headshot. If you don't have the extra money, have a friend take your picture. Be sure to dress up in business attire and have your backdrop be a white wall. Do your best to eliminate shadows from reflecting. Do not crop yourself out of a picture from when you were hanging out with friends. I see it all the time on LinkedIn with a person's picture, and someone's arm is around his or her shoulder. To me, it looks tacky and makes it seem like you really don't care. It somewhat equates to taking a friend on your job interview. That's something you just shouldn't do. Take pride in your professional profile. It's yours, not the group's.
- Research the personal success equation. Once you put this formula together for yourself, you should begin to work your life's purpose to self-fulfill your

Polished

heart's desires to impress upon others for theirs. Our lives are not just ours. We are here for one another to help each other succeed on our journeys in life. Treat your life as a business. You are your personal brand. No one can represent you better than you can. It's important to know what you want and have a plan on how to get it. Take the time to create an ongoing plan to make your life better. The following quote from the Kanye West and Jay-Z remix of "Diamonds of Sierra Leone" speaks directly to treating yourself as a business. "I'm not a businessman. I'm a Business, Man."

- There is a timeless message from Tyler Perry that was posted on YouTube in 2012. Tyler speaks for just under five minutes about the power of focusing on one thing at a time to bring prosperity in your life. Have a listen at https://www.youtube.com/watch?v=xhiuI7u1P7w. Every entrepreneur needs to watch Tyler Perry's success story.
- Check out this interview by Tavis Smiley with Will Smith at https://www.youtube.com/watch?v=JQodPufvdok. Everyone has the quality of leadership. It begins with self. Never let anyone tell you differently. If you cannot lead yourself, how will you lead others? If you lead your life accordingly, others will follow. Most of us have silent followers, people who are too bashful to tell you they like what you are doing and want to learn from you. If you happen to be aware of your surroundings, pay attention to those who seem to be admiring you and offer bits of information to them. That will open them up to becoming open enough to follow you without shame. Develop a relationship with them and mentor them. But also take the time to learn from them. True

leaders learn from their followers just as followers learn from their leaders. Leaders learn how their followers need to be led. They learn how their followers learn and adjust their teaching skills so it is easily adapted. Everyone is a leader. It does not take a leadership position to become a leader. Leaders are recognized before they are given an official leadership position. What do you think gets them into that leadership position? If the CEO or other leader figures laugh at something you don't find funny, make it a point not to guffaw. Most of the time, they are just seeing who is dumb enough to laugh with them. That's how they find out who the leaders of the group are and who the followers are.

- Create a plan for yourself. If you're not already working within your life's passion, start! Learn how to generate revenue for yourself by doing something you love. This will not be work for you. It will be pure pleasure. Not only are you fulfilling your dreams and desires, you are sharing your God-given talents with the world. Understand that your job is always a temporary opportunity. Until you are calling the shots God has designed that are for your life, only then will your works not be temporary. Both of my parents have always hustled. My mom is a nurse by profession. Not only did she work a nine-to-five position, she was a private duty nurse from time to time and was her own boss. Everywhere she goes, she builds relationships with people because she's a go-getter. Now she is running a CNA school for someone who had a vision and put his plan into action. He entrusted my mom with his concept, and she is working it, leveraging her network to make opportunities happen for this business and the students who attend the school. God blessed my mom with networking skills and the ability to pull the right people together to complete projects and opportunities. Once God ordains it, it won't go wrong. You have to work His design. By the time you are reading this, my mom's main plan will be in full swing. She's starting a nonprofit organization for women who are transitioning out of foster care to teach them life skills. My mom's original plan prepared her for this. She also focused on the success of someone else's business, which makes her a triumph. My dad was a graphic design artist by profession. He's worked for a few major corporations, and his most recent was Crown Cork and Seal, one of the world's largest bottle packaging companies. My dad did a lot of freelance work. I've seen him script type in our basement for many years. If you're unfamiliar with the term "script type," it's basically placement of words before books are published. My dad always told me, "You need to have more than one way to make money." He and my mom taught me how to hustle. They both have drive and passion for what they believe in, and they both go hard from the muscle to make it happen.

- After your interviews, send your follow-up messages—emails, handwritten notes, or phone calls—but remember to be patient. If you are told you will hear something by a certain time period and you don't, feel free to reach out to inquire. Sometimes the hiring parties take vacations, have emergencies, or remain busy with other things. I had an interview process start in late June 2012 and did not get a job offer from the company until September that year, the Friday before Labor Day weekend to be exact. Talk about

feeling anxious and patient. That was a roller coaster of emotions. But it taught me that patience is truly a virtue and must be exercised to control the emotional feelings that can be pressed upon you.
- Read. Read articles and books about things you are passionate about. Read the words of other who share your passions. Their point of view will give you another window to look through, which will help keep the fire in your belly ignited. I read a lot of self-help articles and books to keep me going as I move closer to my dreams of helping others move nearer to their dreams. I also enjoy reading articles and books on spirituality. Only you know your heart. God knows it as well. But you are the only being who can walk in your shoes down the path of enlightenment and in the direction your other self will try to guide you. My thoughts on spirituality take me in the direction of my pure beliefs, not dogmas someone has tried to force upon me. I urge you to find yourself as you embark on life. What we have today is not all we have for our lives. And I am not only speaking about material possessions. I'm talking about growth in mind, body, and soul. It's development in your journey to help others walk down a path of betterment for self and others. We are not designed to just help ourselves. We are molded to assist others make their way. We are a team of human beings designed alike but to be different in many ways. No one person can do all things alone. Help has been given to each of us to get to our destinations we set out to reach.
- The owner, CEO, and/or president of the company you work for is not as scary as you think. Spark up a conversation with him or her. You will see he or she

is very interested and happy to have that conversation with you. Build a relationship with him or her. Pick his or her brain. Joke around with him or her. Get to know him or her on a different level outside of the work environment. Make him or her curious about you and wonder so much that he or she starts asking you questions to get to know who you are, where you come from, and where you plan on going. Build relationships with him or her, and make him or her an ally. You never know where that relationship can take you or him or her. And if your coworkers start calling you a suck-up or any other name, just ignore them. You have plans to be more than what you are as an employee. Also be sure to have something to offer back to your newfound allies. They will appreciate that.

- If you feel you are burning out due to work, talk to your supervisor, express your feelings, and schedule some time off. One day usually helps. I like taking a recuperate day on a Wednesday to break up the week. Once I return back to work on Thursday, I am refreshed and ready to go for the next two days. Then the weekend is here. Yes, it's like having two Mondays in a week, but it breaks up your week and allows you to hit the reset button on your brain. Take the time off to regroup and start fresh again. Your supervisor will appreciate your wisdom for recognizing that you are being compromised and consumed by work, which is pushing you to the limits of your stress factor. No one performs at his or her best when being compromised mentally with the day-to-day issues of work wearing him or her down.

- I'm always winning because I'm always giving. I'm always giving advice to people. And I'm always giving my time to those who deserve it. Not everyone deserves your moments. Eventually you will be able to determine whom he or she is. Here's a hint or two: the ones who deserve your time will always show gratitude. The ones who don't will always be the ones who have their hands out.
- Study the events you attend for two reasons: ensure you are dressed properly for the event and find out who will be in attendance so you can make the right connections to help others first and to be helped second.
- Always remember there is life outside work. People only allow you to see what they want you to observe. So if you run into a coworker after working hours and he or she is dressed down in jeans, sneaker, sweats, and so forth, don't act shocked. He or she has regular everyday clothes just like you. Just because you've only seen him or her in business attire does not mean that's all he or she owns and wears. Everybody lets his or her hair down at some point.
- When I was interviewing for a position at Fiberlink Communications, Phil Yurko, Director of Infrastructure of Operations gave me a golden nugget during the interview. He said, "If you become a member of the engineering team, find out who the movers and shakers in the organization are. Those are the people who will get you the answers you need." At that time, I was nineteen years into my IT career. No one has ever given me such great advice. It all came together for me right there. And now when I interview people or have

conversations with those who are looking for jobs, I pass that same nugget along to them.
- After eating, check your face, including your teeth, to ensure no food is left. Also look over your clothes for dropped food. There's nothing more embarrassing than having food in your teeth or crumbs and spills on your clothes while talking to people. Hopefully if you've missed it, someone will be nice enough to inform you. And if you see someone has something in his or her teeth or on their clothes, politely let him or her know so he or she can remove it before anyone else notices.
- Use a lint brush to remove lint from your clothes. And if your clothes have static cling, use Static Guard. Appearance is key.
- Have you ever noticed your shirt collar spread across your chest like a butterfly? A cool product called Wurkin Stiff Collar Stays is a magnetic collar stay that allows your collar to appear stiff and in place. I first saw this on *Shark Tank* when Jon Boos presented his product to the sharks. I immediately began looking for this product and found it on www.wurkinstiffs.com. I purchased a three-pack. Wurkin Stiffs will change your life along with your shirt collar. This is one of the best purchases I ever made to enhance my appearance. I reached out to Jon on LinkedIn and connected with him. I told him how I heard about his product and how much it's changed my appearance. I also told him how I was writing this book and mentioned his product. He wished me luck and much success.
- If you are leaving a company on a good note, ask your direct manager for a letter of recommendation. If you work closely with customers, ask them for a letter as

well. When I worked for First Union as a software implementation specialist, I traveled to customer sites regularly to install our Global Funds Transfer software and train accounting teams on the product. One of my most exciting customers was the Kuwaiti Embassy in Washington, DC. Once I completed my training, I asked the chief accountant if he could write a letter of recommendation to my manager based on my performance. When I arrived back in the office a few days later, I had the letter waiting for me on the letterhead of the Kuwaiti Embassy. Talk about excitement and the possibility of new opportunities to come simply from a letter of recommendation of such a great caliber. From that letter of recommendation and a few others I received over a period of time, I began furnishing them along with my résumé when I went on job interviews. Those letters alone boosted my credibility and helped land new positions in various organizations.

- The person who is all about success for himself or herself may obtain success but only for a short period of time. Someone who is all about the success of others will obtain accomplishment for a lifetime. I cannot stress enough the importance of helping others along the way. The more people you help become successful, the more accomplished you will become. #Payitforward.

CHAPTER 18
SOME BOOKS I'VE READ

Read books and articles that support your passions and others that don't to keep you well-rounded and balanced. If you're like me, sitting still to read a book is difficult due to my schedule. My alternative is audio books. However, I do enjoy taking the time to sit down to read a good book. If you spend a lot of time on the go, download audio books from your favorite distributor, for example, iTunes, Amazon, Audible, and so forth. Here's a list of some of my favorite books I've read.

- *The Holy Bible (King James Version)*
  Jon Acuff

- *Do Over: Rescue Monday, Reinvent Your Work, and Never Get Stuck*
  James Altucher

Calvin Purnell, Jr.

- *Choose Yourself*
  Adam Bryant

- *The Corner Office: Indispensable and Unexpected Lessons from CEOs on How to Lead and Succeed*
  Bob Burg and John David Mann

- *The Go-Giver*
  Rhonda Byrne

- *The Secret*
  Susan Cain

- *Quiet: The Power of Introverts in a World That Can't Stop Talking*
  Grant Cardone

- *The 10X Rule—The Only Difference Between Success and Failure*[3]
  Dale Carnegie

- *How to Win Friends & Influence People*[4]
  George S. Clason

- *Richest Man in Babylon*

---

[3] My friend, Elton Brand, referred this book to me. After reading it, I reached out and connected with Mr. Cardone on LinkedIn. I told him how much I enjoyed reading this book and how it opened my eyes to a 10X lifestyle. Grant responded to my message and sent me an autographed copy of *Sell or Be Sold: How to Get Your Way in Business and Life*. I can't wait to read it.

[4] My friend, Tristan Nunnally, gifted this book to me. He was surprised I hadn't read this book when he first told me about it. He was nice enough to sow a seed in me with it.

Paulo Coelho

- *The Alchemist*

George C. Fraser

- *Click: Ten Truths for Building Extraordinary Relationships*

Chris Gardner

- *The Pursuit of Happyness*

Malcolm Gladwell

- *Blink: The Power of Thinking without Thinking*
- *Outliers: The Story of Success*

Adrian Gostick and Chester Elton

- *The Carrot Principle*[5]

Robert Greene

- *The 48 Laws of Power*
- *Seduction*

Tim S. Grover

- *Relentless*

Darren Hardy

- *The Compound Effect*

---

[5] My friend, Elton Brand, gifted this book to me.

- *Success Magazine*[6]
  Shawn Kent Hayashi

- *Conversations for Change: 12 Ways to Say It Right When It Matters Most*
  Dave Hemsath and Leslie Yerkes

- *301 Ways to Have Fun at Work*
  Napoleon Hill

- *Napoleon Hill in His Own Voice: Rare Recordings of His Lectures*[7]
- *Outwitting the Devil: The Secret to Freedom and Success*[8]

---

[6] I saw Darren speak live in September 2013 in Orlando. He spoke about the *Belief System: What's Holding You Back from Being Successful*. He brought up all great points that I am not going to speak about because I do not have his permission to print his material. I urge you to research Darren. *The Compound Effect* is a great book! *Success Magazine* is a great text that prints real-life success stories from many people. You will benefit from getting a subscription. If you don't want to, just go pick up a copy from a bookstore or order a copy online.

[7] This was ten hours and thirteen minutes of Napoleon Hill's lectures that still are a great benefit to have in my collection of material that has and will continue to help me grow. I urge you to get it. It is available on iTunes.

[8] Mr. Hill's material first touched my life when I read *Outwitting the Devil*. And I have read the book seven times as of December 2, 2013. It is a repeated read for me because, each time I go over it, I find something new that relates to my life and current situation. Napoleon Hill speaks on definiteness of purpose. I won't speak anymore on his teachings because I urge you to read his books. I pray they touch your life in a beneficial way as his material has impacted mine for the better.

- *Think and Grow Rich*
  His Holiness the Dalai Lama

- *The Art of Happiness*

- *How to See Yourself as You Really Are*
  Don Hutson, Ethan Willis, and Ken Blanchard

- *The One Minute Entrepreneur*
  T. D. Jakes

- *Before You Do: Making Great Decisions That You Won't Regret*

- *Reposition Yourself: Living Life without Limits*
  Spencer Johnson

- *Present*

- *Who Moved My Cheese?*
  Willie Jolley

- *A Setback Is a Setup for a Comeback*
  Daniel Kahneman

- *Thinking, Fast and Slow*
  Robert Kiyosaki

- *Rich Dad Poor Dad*
  John C. Maxwell

- Attitude 101

- Everyone Communicates, Few Connect: What the Almost Effective People Do Differently

- Failing Forward: Turning Mistakes into Stepping Stones for Success

- Leadership 101

- The 21 Irrefutable Laws of Leadership

- The 360 Degree Leader

Barack Obama

- The Audacity of Hope: Thoughts on Reclaiming the American Dream

Kerry Patterson, Joseph Grenny, Ron McMillian, Al Switzler, and Stephen R. Covey

- Crucial Conversations: Tools for Talking When Stakes Are High

Randy Pausch and Jeffrey Zaslow

- The Last Lecture

Susan RoAne

- How to Work a Room: Your Essential Guide to Savvy Socializing

- RoAne's Rules: How to Make the Right Impression: What to Say and How to Say It

- *What Do I Say Next?*
  Don Miguel Ruiz

- *The Four Agreements—A Practical Guide to Personal Freedom*
  Richard Stengel

- *Mandela's Way: Fifteen Lessons on Life, Love, and Courage*
  Denzel Washington

- *A Hand to Guide Me*

CHAPTER 19
A FEW PIECES ABOUT ME

You don't know that I am a convicted felon. In 2003 I was convicted on an aggravated assault charge with a firearm. No one was physically harmed. It was just one day of not thinking. Prior to that conviction, I was a white-collar worker in IT.

All my life, I've heard people say, "Convicted felons can never get good jobs." Well, I'm here to tell you it's far from the truth. It may take a few years before you can get a better job, but it is possible. #trusttheprocess

Several organizations hire convicted felons to give them a second chance. Many people make mistakes and deserve to be given opportunities to get their lives back in order. I've been blessed to have the chance to reestablish my career. If ever faced with being a deciding factor of a convicted felon, have some compassion, but don't be naïve. Do some research on his or her track record and ask what he or she has done to rehabilitate himself or herself.

Polished

I took the time to get to know myself and understand what my flaws are. I told myself that I would never put my family or myself through the stress again of being incarcerated. With that said, I entered psychological therapy to gain control over the anger issues I had. I spent five years in anger management therapy to help understand and control those issues.

That is why I stress upon you to understand who you are and take the time to know you and all of the flaws you possess. You cannot allow people or things to push you to a limit that is uncontrollable. We should always be in control of ourselves. The last thing you want is for someone else telling you when to wake up, eat, and see your loved ones. Know your worth. Know you.

In May 2012, the Federal Bureau of Prisons asked me to be a part of a discussion panel as an ex-offender with celebrity chef, Chef Jeff. I had the opportunity to tell my story of how I beat the odds and reestablished my life after incarceration. We fielded questions from the ex-offenders in the audience who wanted to know what it took to become reestablished into society after prison.

When I was asked to be a part of the panel, I saw this as one of many ways for me to #payitforward. I did not hesitate to accept the opportunity. At the end of the program, we were able to interact with the audience. I took that as a chance to further encourage some of the men and women I spoke to.

Reentry is not an easy process. And by no means do I try to make it seem as if it is a cakewalk. It is far from it. Every time I go on job interviews, I first tell the interviewer, "I have a felony conviction on my record. If this is going to be a problem for the organization, I truly understand and do not want to waste your time going forward."

Calvin Purnell, Jr.

Some interviewers were up front with me by thanking me for my honesty and letting me know that it would be a problem. Some would tell me it was not an issue and moved forward with the interview. The key is to be able to keep pushing forward to get past all the time we hear no. You have to learn to not take it personal. It's hard not to, but you have to learn. You must realize that you made the mistake and sometimes there is a price to pay after you've paid your debt to society.

I received this certificate for participating in the panel discussion for ex-offenders. And below the certificate is a picture of Chef Jeff and me.

Certificate of Appreciation

This certificate is presented to

Calvin Purnell

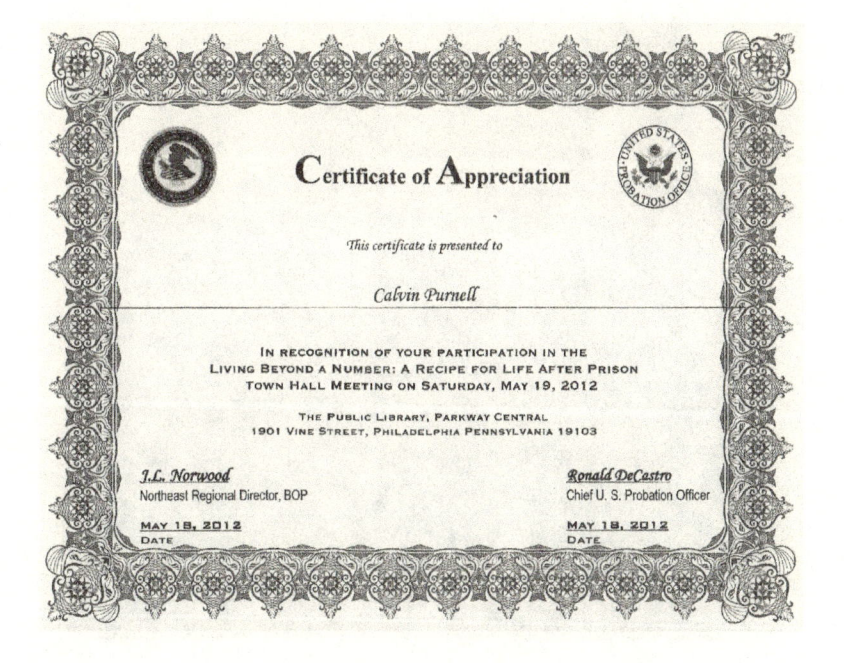

IN RECOGNITION OF YOUR PARTICIPATION IN THE
LIVING BEYOND A NUMBER: A RECIPE FOR LIFE AFTER PRISON
TOWN HALL MEETING ON SATURDAY, MAY 19, 2012

THE PUBLIC LIBRARY, PARKWAY CENTRAL
1901 VINE STREET, PHILADELPHIA PENNSYLVANIA 19103

J.L. Norwood
Northeast Regional Director, BOP
MAY 18, 2012
DATE

Ronald DeCastro
Chief U. S. Probation Officer
MAY 18, 2012
DATE

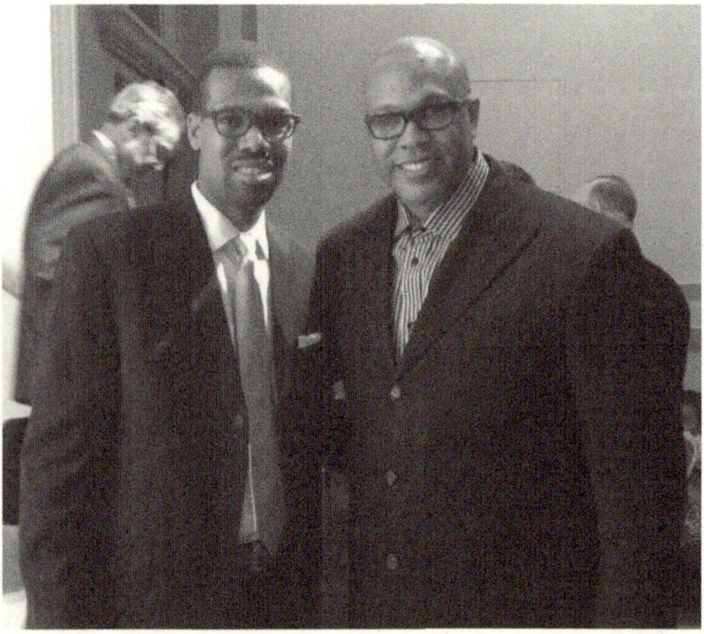

Also due to my parents' teachings, not only do I have a career in IT, I also cut hair. One year for Christmas, my dad gave me a pair of clippers. He told me to learn how to cut hair because he was tired of giving me money. I was fifteen years old at the time. So I started out cutting my buddies' hair. Over time I became pretty darn good at it. To this day, I have another source to make money if needed.

Do you remember my good friend Shawn (Shizz) Porter? Let's just say he definitely looks out for me when celebrities travel to the Philadelphia area and need haircuts. If you're ever in need of a personal barber and my time permits, reach out to me. I just might be able to come through and cut your hair. House calls only!

Finally, if you have Instagram and want some more inspiration in your life, feel free to follow me. My IG name is MindfullySpeaking. I post daily devotionals, motivational quotes, my personal style, and pictures of food every now and again.

I hope this book has been a blessing to you as it's been to me for writing it. Please feel free to email me with any questions you may have regarding this book or if you are looking for a mentor. We can interview each other to see if we are a good fit for one another. In all seriousness, email me at polishedthebook@gmail.com. I will do my best to respond in a timely manner.

I encourage you to keep going in your career, your passions, and life. We are all designed to create something. What that is for you, only you and God know right now. So bring it to life so everyone else will know too! Take your passions personally. Pray about them, and ask God to give you the guidance you need to complete your assignments given to you. Do not waste your talents.

God granted you with gifts. Find a way to capitalize on them and gift them away. Yes, gift them away.

I prayed for this! Thank you, God!

REFERENCES

Butler, R. "Era of the Gentleman: Upscale Grooming Is the New Trend Among Men of All Ages." *Jet* 117(60): 28.

Obama, B. *Audacity of Hope: Reclaiming the American Dream.* Crown Publishing, 2006.

Stengle, R. *Mandela's Way: Lesson on Life, Love and Courage.* Crown Archetype, 2010.

Zimmerman, M. "Ties that Bind." *Success Magazine* (November 2012): 50–55.

Made in the USA
Coppell, TX
26 July 2023